FARRAGO

My Humble Forays into the
Pathways of Bereavement

PRINCE BALEKE

Prince Baleke Inc

Copyright © 2022 PRINCE BALEKE

All rights reserved

The characters and events portrayed in this book are fictitious. Any similarity to real persons, living or dead, is coincidental and not intended by the author.

No part of this book may be reproduced, or stored in a retrieval system, or transmitted in any form or by any means, electronic, mechanical, photocopying, recording, or otherwise, without express written permission of the publisher.

ISBN-13: 9798420451199

Cover design by: Prince Baleke Inc
Library of Congress Control Number: 2018675309
Printed in the United States of America

PREFACE

The bond with a loved one is powerfully strong, so strong, that when you reconnect with that person who meant the world to you after many years of being apart, it has a different type of energy, and to lose them then is the worst pain anyone can ever feel. But before I go in too deep about it, there's something I need first to clear off my chest.

It was a question, someone, I value most in my life asked me; "how does it feel to talk about your grieving experience finally?"

"Recounting the story feels like an elephant taking its feet off my chest," I added in response.

PROLOGUE

I have been on a long journey of self-healing and self-discovery for twelve solid years. I refused to follow people's opinions, adverse effects and peer pressure. I disconnect from anyone who doesn't serve my purpose or deposit anything meaningful but only withdraw to dim my shine. Before the pilgrimage, I always tried to force love where it didn't belong. I thought I would find it in other people but ended up being heartbroken, used, and left to hang because I trusted way too much and gave a billion per cent to phoney ass people; I thought loved me and gave myself nada. Well! Life can be a shitty show at times. The saddest thing about putting all your trust in people and positioning their needs before your own is that you get nothing in return or end up being disappointed. Not that I do good deeds to be glorified and televised, but it's a good feeling to know your efforts are appreciated, and it can be downsizing when taken for granted. Some people don't understand the value of friendship, one of the hardest lessons I had to teach myself was that; learning how to love you is the first step to discovering the true meaning of love. Self-discovery has helped me to identify my abilities, how to leverage and develop them. With self-discovery, you come to accept yourself more and start caring less about other people's approval. Self-discovery makes you more comfortable with who you are, which tends to push people away. You become stronger at heart and, as with any muscle, the more you exercise, the more it strengthens. Society has somehow made you believe that you must confide in someone else to comprehend love. Or, for you to look beautiful, you have to wear makeup, to a point where you've to sneak out of the bedroom in the middle of the night to fix your face and quickly get back to bed before your one-night stand or boyfriend wakes up. That seems like a full-time job on top of your actual paying job, but who am I to judge another human being? Some women wear wigs on top of their natural hair to look prettier; understandably, you might not have enough time to brush your hair, but it would be best to walk freely without makeup, fake nails, or an extra extension of eyelashes. Something you do to please a man or woman who will even leave you for someone lower than your standards or cheat on you, after going through all that hard work of shining bright like a diamond to please them. Tell me:

- ✓ Young woman, what's wrong with your looks?
- ✓ Youngman who taught you how to hate yourself?
- ✓ Youngman, why do you constantly shave your beard bold?
- ✓ Young woman, what's wrong with having short fingernails?
- ✓ Young woman, what's wrong with having some meat on your body?
- ✓ Why do you've to work out tirelessly for six-packs to look more appealing?

While there are fewer people in your life, those who

choose to leave are the most critical ones that tend to force their agendas on you and are usually negative. Try to distance yourself from such individuals and replace them with people who genuinely love you for who you naturally are. Don't be afraid to lose someone who doesn't add to your being; it won't even matter if they add to scars received from prior experiences. Live freely without having to hide who you are, and anyone who's not comfortable with that, tell them politely to 'f****k off. People will come from different walks of life to specifically test you. Some will want to see if you love them more than "self." It's not a bad thing; use that as an incentive to help you learn and discover more about yourself because the reality of it is that! When you become part of the universe, the universe becomes part of whom you love, and that should be you. There's no pain you go through that wasn't meant for you by your creator. You are not the first person to experience a pain so deep that makes you feel that suffocating heat, and you're most definitely not the only one going through uncomfortable times. When you feel like life's flushing you down the toilet, and everything of yours is draining down with you. Stop wheezing for air, inhale that shit, and eat that shit too because it's not a calling card to the end of life. It's a process you go through before reaching the top. Look up at trees; for instance, they lose all their leaves every autumn, and they remain standing tall, waiting for better days to come ahead. Trees don't fall on people because their leaves are blown in the wind or drop branches onto people's houses to show how devastated they are. And they surely don't scream in anger while you pass them by or boo you like bogeyman to scare the crap out of you. You spend tearful nights crying your heart to sleep, in other words, wondering what you can do to put someone else first. Some people don't even pay you attention or pay for your hair or nails to get done; they still expect you to look good when they get back home and tell you, you need to put more effort in but still tell you you're too made up that it's all too much and you don't look good, so then once you take it all off, you still don't look good enough and don't put the effort in anymore. The narcissists use this to break you down to control you emotionally, so nothing you do is good enough for them, and you keep trying to win their approval. When you look in the mirror and see that reflection staring back at you, look at them eye to eye and speak this into existence; you are beautiful, imaginative, cared for and can be loved unconditionally by someone who understands how worthy you are. You have been through hell; you believed all the lies told against you that you are unlovable; you doubted yourself and have taken the blame and carried the burden for far too long. They called you a worthless piece of shit, and they convinced you that if you were to commit suicide, no one would miss you when you're gone. You have lost hope that no one will ever be able to love you right because you are bedding or have bedded an antagonist, and all they ever fed you was a heap load of shit. But, guess what? There is someone special out there, waiting on the other side of your pain, and all they ever do is to pray for you to stop beating yourself up. So, the sooner you get your act together, the quicker they will come to you with open, loving arms. Now! You may be doubting this manifestation and questioning who that mysterious lover might be?

When the time is right, love will call you by your birth name. You will become overjoyed, and sometimes you will find yourself smiling because someone can finally give you a flutter of butterflies in your stomach. But, before you get there, you will first have to learn how to love yourself and let everything be all about you. You have taken the first step, which was to walk away from those who don't see your worth or serve the same purpose as you. However, the second step won't be a walk in the park or a stroll to the shops; it will feel like a journey to hell and back. Therefore, as soon as you learn how to love yourself, you will discover that; when someone truly loves you, they love all of you, not only when lights go down to deep throats and choking modes. And most definitely, you shouldn't care about how your hair looks like whether you've got some makeup on or whether your eyelashes are on point. If someone wants you, they should love the shit out of you regardless. Your heart and mind are meant to work together. When you're detached from your heart, the mind resists change. The mind identifies with our beliefs, and without the guidance of the heart, it becomes fearful and defensive, and when it is questioned, it goes into lock-down. Change originates in the heart, and the heart teaches the mind. The nature of your heart is love, and love has no past, present, or future; it simply is. As your heart creates new beliefs based on love and respect, your emotions update, and your mind relaxes. Your truth overwrites the old lies, and bonds of relationship strengthen. You create a deeper understanding of yourself that reflects your relations with others. Your natural curiosity returns as you learn how your mind works and how to love yourself. When you can't help but wonder, what it would be like if you don't feel drained, unloved or even respond with anguish the old way? Your creativity comes to its feet and applauds. We can imagine our transformed future in the present time and feel the feelings and emotions of our healed state going forward. Curiosity isn't easily stopped; throughout the day, you find yourself wondering, what it would be like to truly fall in love and, at that moment, you are further unbound to the problem; you are writing a new story, and your mind and body feel it. A curious mind and an active imagination are strong medicine. They move you along the healing path and towards whatever goal you set.

What causes self-doubt is falling for the wrong person, out of desperation, loneliness, and most importantly, before you can truly understand what love is all about and the fact that everything in life has become too complicated and competitive in a misleading way. I never knew true love until I first learnt how to 'love myself'Before I found myself, I used to love others hard, and I poured everything I had into them without blinking an eye. Not knowing, I had to first deposit all that fetish love into me before sharing it with anyone else. You will climb mountains searching for someone to love you, and unfortunately, you will end up knocking on rocks or the wrong doors. This doesn't classify you as stupid because it's all part of the healing process until you learn how to do it right. The person who deserves to be loved most has been living right next to you all along. So, let love be about one person at the beginning, and after that, let it spread through your veins, and thrive underneath your skin before you can share it with others. If you are among those who seek to find love from someone else, you are facing the wrong direction and looking in the wrong places. I suggest you change direction in due course before time leads you to regrets. At some point, you have witnessed someone afraid of Mondays that they even dream of sipping a big cup of coffee on a Sunday evening to kick start their Monday morning. If they think waking up to a Monday morning full of tasks is alarming, you should let them know that it is a piece of cake for people who learned how to love themselves the hard way. Discovering how to love a damaged you is the most challenging task anyone can face as you go through a lot, but it's a pilgrimage worth taking in the end. When you learn how to love yourself, you start appreciating the little things in your life and everyone around you. Before I discovered myself, I always thought finding a partner out of desperation would make me feel whole. But little did I know, I had to first discover a loving yourself before searching for my other half. I have known several people who knew what love was, and I almost believed them. In simple terms, we all lived under one roof of the inexperienced about love, and we didn't even know it. That did mean I was stupid or useless, and those I met alongside my journey of self-discovery, no. It means I was a human being who didn't know better but theoretically thought I knew everything. On the other hand, society has played a significant role in giving people the wrong ideas of almost everything. We look at what celebrities have, and we think we can have that tainted love they play in fiction movies and series, but in reality, you live alone with maybe a needy cat or next to a neighbour with a Samoyed dog barking 52.8 times every day. Living in the unknown has left many people lonely, and they don't even know it. We keep on competing against each other stupid and aimless things when we should all divide and conquer. Society has caused more confusion in people's heads than anything. What we think is love because someone famous is doing it is sickening to the core of my soul. We have somehow lost hope in everything because we're not used to thinking for ourselves. Love is overrated. Swiping apps have become our dating agents, and I guess I should slightly blame it on technology. But I won't because I will again drive back to society.

Don't get me wrong, I am a lover of technology, not a fighter of its advancement, as, since its invasion, it has made so many things 'simpler' if that's the appropriate English word to use. Are you familiar with the saying; when you have something, you don't know the value it possesses until it's gone, then you miss the presence of it. You don't need a reason to love or be loved, and if you have the power to put a smile on someone else's face, do it in a heartbeat because in this crappy society we live in, someone somewhere needs it more than you think you do. However, don't let that make you feel putting yourself first is selfish; it's necessary. The world will judge you no matter how good or bad you believe you are, so live your life the way you please or want to. Because to attract better, you have to become better yourself. You can't do the same things and expect to see different results. Stop blaming everyone for how bad things turn out or how others treat you. It's time to take full responsibility for your actions by altering your mindset, upgrading your old habits and being more positive. Unfuck yourself back to whom you were before the bad dimmed your fucking shine. And when manifesting, ensure you express gratitude now because your desires are already yours if you believe they are yours. When you have faith, the universe has your back.

A grateful heart is a magnet for blessings, so give thanks now for your manifestations. Self-love isn't just about loving the person you are; it's also about appreciating how far you have come and what you have achieved along the lines. Self-love is the greatest middle finger to those who undermine your inner beauty, potential and anyone who has ever mistreated you. It's, therefore, important to spend time alone sometimes to reflect upon and meet your own needs in a way that will help you understand what makes you tick. Self-love doesn't imply your selfish; it takes a lot of work for someone to learn the person there, so when you increase the voltage of your watts to a higher percentage than the dimmed light people are used to seeing. Those who can't handle the brightness of your light consider Self Love selfish. It's not a crime to choose differently from the usual, and if possible, you should increase the voltage even higher and say to yourself, 'I'm not a people pleaser'. Then love the shit out of you to a point where your mood doesn't shift based on other people's insignificant actions. Self-love is a must because when you self-regulate, you're able to control the trajectory of your emotions and resulting actions based on your values and a sense of purpose. Align your personality with your soul in everything you do and ensure to put yourself first, then grow so remarkably that people have to get to know you all over again. You have been accepting people to treat you like a doormat, and you continued to let it happen because you expected them to make you feel happy. Your authenticity is the medicine you need to step out of your comfort zone. The power is in your hands, and it's entirely up to you to put a stand to someone else's dense stands. No one will ever love you the way you can love yourself, and the same applies to making you happy. It's not someone else's job to make all this happen. If you think so, then you've been doing it the wrong way.

Now, this might sound a bit deceitful, but it's a fact.

Happiness is an inside job, which starts with Self Love. You will come to realise one day that your happiness was never someone else's job. Marrying someone who's financially free but the saddest person alive is like being in a relationship with someone who promises to love you to the moon and back when their intentions are facing you at the gates of hell. I will love you to the moon ...blah.... blah. It is the phoniest saying someone uses when they've just wanted a taste of your fruit, and as soon as the going gets tough, they fail to reflect upon empty promises, and it always ends in breaking up or slapping your face with divorce papers or lawsuits. Happiness is not a told fairytale story of losing one shoe on your way to a party, expecting a Prince Charming to pick it up and come looking for you in your local suburbs. And has never been about following the footsteps of those before you; it has been your calling all along. When you start valuing yourself more, you will discover that happiness is about self-discovery. Pay more attention to the beating of your heart and follow your intuition, as it never lies. Happiness is about being much kinder to yourself. It's about embarrassing the person you are becoming and learning how to live underneath the skin of the person you were born to be, but never in the hands of someone else. It has always been about you, and it will continue to be so until your last breath. If I were to go back and undo all my mistakes, I would obliterate myself. My second beloved mother told me that; you first fall before learning how to walk. Something we have all done at a certain point in our upbringing, and we still keep at it until the day we die. If you don't know how to love who you are deep down, what you feel towards someone isn't love.

Not until you learn to love the person who needs nurturing. You will always walk a milestone of breakups. When you are still young, you unknowingly take many good things and important people for granted because you think you know better. But in reality, you are still in the process of learning how to do something. I have acknowledged now that; I was way too late to be in my mother's life for me to save her from dying. I have made way too many mistakes, and I missed out on so many chances I shouldn't have taken for granted. I guess I am just like everyone else, in which we are all human beings in the end. You can't control everything that happens to you, and you can never avoid making mistakes. The only thing you can do is learn from whichever mistake, amend your old ways and leave with it. My biggest regret in life is; I wish I had looked for my mother sooner. Maybe, I would've prevented her death. Things would've been different from the way they're now. I could've bonded with my late mother more and she could've lived to see her grandchildren grow, go to school and may've seen them walk down the aisle. Or I wish I understood the actual definition of life than I do now. Or I wish I had the knowledge I have now and I was located where I am now.

This book is dedicated to
all my readers grieving
the loss of a parent, friend,
pet, possession and job.

My life hasn't been so easy as falling off a log, but I guess it's the process we all go through. While facing life tribulations, and being punched in the face in every direction you turn your face. I always took things lightly, because I had hope that things can get better in time. I never understood death growing up as a child. Sadly enough, I used to hear people say they have lost someone. I cried alongside their families while they mourned the loss of their loved ones, and it never occurred to me to ask how they felt. But I guess I was young, naive and didn't care much or feel empathy for their feelings. As I started growing the heck up, people closest to me, like my three beloved grandmothers, a lovable wise uncle who worked at the Ugandan Airport, and my granddad who didn't talk much, started falling off the family tree, followed by three of my best friends. I somehow felt the pain caused by death, but it was still not close until I lost my mother. I came to understand what death

ntirely. I wept more tears than I had ever when
my ass whipped by my father for being stubborn. Pure
heartfelt tears, unanswered questions, and a heavy storm
of pain in my chest like an elephant had its giant foot all
over me. On a sad note, not spending much time with my
mother the way it should've or like any child would've
spent quality time with their mother made the situation
way too extreme. The most agonising moment was that I
didn't get an opportunity to ask her the crucial question
every confused child would ask a long time missed parent; "why did you leave me behind?"

My beloved mother's death left me confused and heartbroken to the point that it took me a long while to realise she wasn't coming back from that long sleep. I went to her grave a couple of times to try and understand why she had to leave me when I needed her most. This pain had built up from the moment we got separated. I don't know why my father separated us, but I certainly recall having an excellent bond with my mother. She was the lead singer at a famous church in Nankulabye, a local suburb of Mengo, where she went every day for church choir rehearsals, and given she didn't have a babysitter. She always took me everywhere she went, and she was so proud calling me her little Prince charming at the age of five. She had an angelic voice whenever she opened her mouth to sing alongside her choir members. She was someone with a big loving heart and way too kind. She was selfless and put other people first like Jaheim put that woman first. She was someone who put other people's needs before hers and wanted to see everyone smiling. Her death took the other part of me. I hopefully held on so tight, knowing she's somewhere happy and loved the same way she loves big. Deep down, I knew that one day we would unite again and continue from where we left off at the age of five. I wanted to meet my mother so bad but kept on responding when to start the journey, and the more I procrastinated, the little did I know death was planning to step a big elephant foot into our reunion. Now you might be asking yourself why it took me so long to look for my beloved mother?

I procrastinated a lot because we were told growing up that; it's not a good sign to go and visit your parents empty-handed. I, therefore, wanted to make enough money to enable me to buy my mother anything she wanted, given that I didn't know the state of condition she was in. My second mother, whom I always pray God nourishes with nothing but blessings, loved me like her own. I could see she was trying to reunite the both of us, but she couldn't challenge my father's decisions that kept my mother and me apart for all long. Even though I had people who loved me regardless, I was too blind to recognise them because I always had something missing: mother and son love. She taught me to the best of her ability, and she even attempted to take me to see my mother in the 1990s twice. When my beloved second mother took me to see mom, I wanted to run and hide so later I could go back to my mother. I somehow sensed something and thought to myself; "maybe she doesn't want to live with me due to circumstances?"

When my plan to escape from my father failed, I gave in to failure and just remained calm and waited for that moment when I grew a much big brain and went out on an independent adventure to look for my biological mother. From that day on, as a child, I always asked for one thing, which was to grow much more significant, get a job and make enough money to buy my mom enough staff to last her for a very long time, and then go on an adventure of finding my mother. When I say I learnt a valuable lesson from that experience. Believe me, because it's something I don't want my children ever to go through. I realised that there would never be enough money to please your parents in the long run. A little visit does the magic. All a parent wants for their children is to be happy and that they are doing well in life, and you're healthy; the rest is a bonus. But as desperate as I was to please the mother, I became consumed by making enough money even to recognise this. The first impression meant everything to me because she hadn't seen me since I was five years old. Little did I know physical presence means everything to parents because as they grow old, fancy things don't even mean a thing anymore. When I finally got off my ass, I looked for a job. I found one to work as a Customer Service Representative, right in the middle of Kampala City Centre, at a family friend's shop, Genuine Electronics Ltd, where I spoke a salesman's language sold home appliances to people. We made a killing off the things we sold like TV Antennas, DVD players and much more. I worked at Genuine Electronics for quite some time until I woke up one day, feeling energetic to go nowhere other than on an unplanned adventure I promised myself from when I was six years old. I was laid in bed thinking to myself; "this is it."

I have been waiting for this day for decades. I am responsible enough now, and I can do pretty much anything without asking for my father's permission, and there won't be anyone worried about how I was going to cross the road on traffic lights. I went on and on for hours while exercising what to say when I found my mom. Funny enough, I even had the audacity of writing three pages of questions to ask when I saw her. So, on the 26th of June 2006, I dressed up in delight and went out on an adventure to find my mother. I knew exactly where to start and whom to run for directions. Which was the last place I lived with her and where to go next just in case she wasn't there. In Uganda, we have Bajaj motorcycles, Ugandans nicknamed (Boda, Boda) imported from India used as a quicker means of transport to dodge traffic when running late for work or a meeting. I hopped on one because I felt like I was running out of time the more I waited. I took the 'Boda' from Makindye, where I lived to Nankulabye, Mengo, where I last lived with my birth mother and her late parents, whom I found to be the most challenging people I have ever known. They were lovely people who didn't take bullshit in a sense. Sadly, they died before I could properly get to know them more. So, I asked the motorcyclist guy if he knew where I wanted him to take me, and it turned out he also grew in the same area as me, and he even knew my mother's mother. I didn't even bother negotiating the price because I was too desperate to get there on time. I jumped on the Boda, and we took off through Entebbe road's morning traffic. As we continued with the journey, he suggested not to pass within the city centre because of congestion, and I politely said; "I have already put my trust in you. So, whatever you think of will do."

He rode the Boda, Boda, as fast as he could and we brunched off Katwe, and we passed uphill on (King Ronald II Road), and he went around the Buganda Kingdom's Palace to CBS the King's Radio station, and before I knew it, we were on Hoima, Road) where the traffic wasn't as bad as it was on Entebbe Road. Before the Ugandan Government decided to build flyovers to reduce morning and evening traffic, the rush hour traffic was more stressful. I looked at many cars stuck in traffic, and I quietly said to myself; "F******K Me."

You know that blood pumping feeling you get when you're rushing to get somewhere, but traffic won't let you get there on time. You then wish you could grow wings and fly to your destination. I had too many of those thoughts, but I had no other alternative better than to wait until we reached Nankulabye, Mengo, where I last lived with my biological mother. Whist sitting on the Boda, Boda thinking of the unthinkable magic I wasn't born with, a woman in her mid-50s opened the door to get out of a moving taxi, and it opened right in a motorcyclist's passenger's face, who was right in front of us. My heart thumped like it was about to dislocate from its socket. I felt my pulse in my abdominal aorta, the main artery that carries blood from the heart to the rest of the body. Then runs from the heart, down the centre of the chest, and into the abdomen. It's usually customary to feel the blood pumping through this large artery from time to time, but right then, it was the terror of the accident. For a second, I thought to myself; "what if that was me?"

The poor woman's head had blood all over it, with her teeth heavily knocked out. The Matatoo driver fled the scene to God knows where and why he had to run when what happened was by mistake. People were chanting loudly in confusion, which caused confusion and akavuyo that caused further delay in the traffic. Commuters got out without paying, and they walked off while the injured woman was fighting for her life. A good samaritan rushed the woman to the hospital on a Boda, Boda, but I hardly doubt she made it there, alive, because the incident was terrifying and gross to watch. I then looked in the small mirror on my left with this strange feeling that made me believe I was going to see my mother that day, while the other part of my mind was wondering whether to cancel the adventure and head back to keeping busy. While the voice of hope was also motivating me not to give up the fight, I, therefore, continued with the journey, and before I knew it, we were at the house where I last saw my birth mother before my father took me to live with him. I knew the house well, and it was still in the same condition I left it at the age of five. I paid the Boda, Boda man and thanked him for his time, patience and good service; "bambi! Webalenyo. Nsimywe, nyo. Nsimidedala."

"Tewali buzibu, papa, at the end of the day, Tulibaluganda." The Boda, Boda man replied as I handed him a fifty thousand Ugandan shilling note to pay with total satisfaction to deduct thirty thousand because I was more than happy with his outstanding customer service throughout. He thanked me again with gratitude, and as he was handing me my balance back, I said to him; "Tofayo kumpa change, mukume."

"Singabulijjo nvuga bakastoma ngagwe! Bambi, Webalenyo." The Boda, boda man responded.

I was truly happy with the gentleman's services and I told him; "Lindako ndabe obaninamu ezekyemisana."

I checked the other side of the pocket and topped up the change he was handing me with a Ugandan Shillings Tena and said to him; "you're the man."

When the Boda, Boda man left, I stood in front of the house where I last lived with my beloved mother before the separation. And while I was still there starring at the building, I was struck by an overwhelming strange feeling of regret mixed with unforgettable memories we shared with her parents. I then felt sadness for the absence in which we could have created many more everlasting memories—followed by constant thoughts of regret for taking so long to look for my beloved mother. We romanticise our plans but dread the execution. But the reality of things is that the magic we're looking for is in the dirty work we're avoiding. For years, the temptation to look for my biological mother procrastinated until the power struggle played itself out. I was too caught up with making enough money that I forgot the longer it took me to face my biggest fears; Allah was also planning a remarkable journey for my mother. However, not that I was terrified of my mother. My concern was that she might ignore or reject me. Something that might have kept me from missing out to find a good woman to marry. I see some good ones daily, but I become afraid of being rejected. I thought the same thing might happen when I found my biological mother because she knew where I was growing up, but she didn't come to check up on me. Something that made me think she abandoned me and didn't care about me anymore. I thought she was like these women who get a second chance in life, and they decide to cut out their kids not to lose a second marriage and then she leaves her flesh and blood to be the responsibility of the man she got divorced or separated from the past. Blame me for feeling this type of way. And as innocent as I was, she left me no choice other than the one where I had to come up with my own thoughts and imagination of the story behind their break-up.

I was utterly confused for not knowing what happened between the two, which made my mother forget about me like I didn't exist at all. I was young puzzled, devastated about the separation, and even though I was cherished with love by those I grew up with, deep down inside was this sad and lonely child longing for a mother's true love. Even though I was raised by an extraordinary second mother who looked after me as her flesh and blood, it didn't feel the same as it would've been if it was my biological mother. I always felt like a piece of me was missing from my life. Don't get me wrong! Not that I'm not appreciative of what I had at the moment of need; it was what it was, I guess. If you have someone special in your life, let it be your best friend or family member you haven't seen for a long time. I want you to know that it's never unduly late to pay someone special a visit. Right after the thought train departed, I walked to the door and knocked more than twice, but there wasn't any reply. I looked through the window and it seemed like there wasn't anyone at home. I went to the shop ten feet away, to see if they can help me with my quest and found there a salesman in his mid-fifties. He was sat down reading newspapers in one hand with holding a metallic mug of tea in the other hand.

"Mukulu, gyebaleko?" I greeted the shop attendant.

"Kale thebbo. Na, Na, nawegyebale. Mmm! Mba, mbaddee nkwataganye. Nkuyaaaaaambemuki, thebbo?" He uttered with a stammer.

"Njankuyita mubwangu nga omusezi asikula omulambo." I replied jokingly.

"Tukwila kunsonga. Nku, nkuyambe muki?" The shop attendant added.

"Nnonya omukyala omulokole eyabelanga munyumba ekulilanye." I said.

"Enyumba ngabagitunda dda eyo." He responded.

"Omanyi abalibabelamu gyebadda?" I asked.

"Siyinza kulimba. Gezako kunamba yamugandawe." He answered.

"Silina nambaye." I curiously added.

She immediately called me their own Boda, Boda man who knew where the shop was, and without hesitation, he took me to the place that wasn't that far. My biological mother's sister was someone I hadn't seen for a very long time. They came from being the best of friends to I don't know what exactly happened to them. She never came home while I was still living with my biological mother because each time she came around. They ended up arguing about sisterly things I was too young to even understand at the age of five. I think this happens a lot anywhere in the world. When one child is loved most by their parents, the rest of the siblings take it on that child because they feel that child is more special than they are. I became nervous when I sat on the Boda, Boda, to a point where my palms started sweating because I didn't know where to start from and how to express my anger without being disrespectful or sounding too desperate. When we got there, the Boda man and my mom's sister seemed to know each other well. She welcomed us with both hands. She sat us down served us two bottles of soda and these delicious cap cakes. My mother's sister kept on saying; "abaffe, Mutabani! Ngansanyuse okukulabako. Nakulotako enaku zetukubye emabegako. Kumbe olimukubo ogya."

"Byebigelebino." I replied.

"Yekambuze. Maama wo wamukyaliddeko dda?" She asked.

"Nsokeddewuwo mukuluwe, ndyokenzileko ewa maama." I added.

"Omanyigyabela?" She asked.

"Kibuzokilungi nyo enkyo! Naye amazima galinti, simanyi gyabela. Ogedda kunyamba ondagilileyo." I jokingly added not to sound desperate.

"Ngatuvudde mukusaga, omanyigyabela?" She asked.

"Yemuntu gwendudde okulaba."

She looked at me surprised, and she took an intense breath like she was relieved of a heavy burden. I noticed how strange she was acting, and I went with the floor because I wanted her to point me in the right direction. I, therefore, refrained from asking why she seemed so relieved to hear I hadn't seen my mother yet. Shortly, she went to the back of the shop, and she spent almost half an hour there. I wasn't concerned about why given that I was in good hands and that my guts believed she knew where my biological mother was. She eventually returned with written instructions she handed over to the Boda, Boda man, who then rode me to where they thought my birth mother lived. When we reached the place, the Boda man didn't know the exact door, and he didn't know how my mother looked. So, on dropping me, he just pointed me in the direction of many houses where I went door to door asking neighbour from neighbour. The first person I unluckily asked was an enemy to my mother, but before then, I didn't know. However, I noticed the strange vibes she gave me when I described my mother to her. She pretended she didn't know who the person was when she did. She kept me going in circles for almost an hour. I had to explain myself over and over again. She was a professional sorceress who sensed how desperate and helpless I was to find my mother. She tapped into my weakness, and she manipulated that to take a piss out of me. When I came to realise, she wasn't being helpful, I told her; "Kangezeko ewadako."

When I was about to walk out of the door, she gave me an evil look that almost made me piss my pants, that the only nerve I had left in me was to sit my black ass down. On settling down quietly, she poured me a glass of passion fruit, which I rejected right away. She kissed her teeth at me in disgust, and she walked away, stamping her feet heavily onto the floor like a pissed off elephant. I could see the anger of disappointment in her eyes, but I remained calm not to say anything funny to upset her even more because I needed her to help more than she was looking forward to getting on my last nerve. When I refused the drink she offered, I actually thought she was going to consume it herself, but she instead poured the entire glass into one of the flower pots in the sitting room. Shockingly enough, as soon as the soil absorbed the drink, the plant weakened and dried up flowers started dropping off it one by one, right in front of my eyes. That freaked the shit out of me that I almost pissed my pants, and as scary as it seemed, I silently said to myself; "Dear lord! That would have been me on the roast."

I remember, one of my grandmothers told me a story about a jealous woman who gave her husband's born outside child poison in a cocktail of soft drinks because the little boy always came back from school with straight A's. In contrast, her own child returned with poor class performance, lousy behaviour reports, uncompleted assignments, and poor attendance. Thus, considering how fast the flowers deteriorated, that was freaky enough to scare the crap out of any living soul. When I learned she wasn't helpful, I walked out without asking for any further directions. She looked at me pissed, and she kissed her teeth at me, but I didn't give a rat's ass about what she thought. Luckily enough, as soon as I walked out, the neighbour next door to the sorcerer walked out simultaneously. She was tall, dark-skinned and beautiful, just like I remembered how my biological mother looked like the last time I saw her at the age of five. She was holding about three plates with utensils inside three piled up glasses. We both looked at each other, and fire of hope spiked into my heart. We both opened our mouths to say something, and we gave up before words came out. We were both afraid to show excitement, not to be disappointed, because we both had one thing in common: being afraid of rejection. I sneakily looked at her to see if she had a thin black spot on her left cheek before confirming she was the one. It wasn't easy spotting that as she unintentionally kept on moving around a lot. I diverted from finding the spot on her face, and I uncovered other things that checked out in the long run, but again, I couldn't ask someone I hadn't confirmed whether she had a black spot on one of her cheeks or whether she was my biological mother. I, therefore, stood there like a dog that had just lost a bone not to appear creepy to someone I had just met. I felt like giving up, and as I was just about to put an end to my staring contest. I accidentally glimpsed the black spot on one of her cheeks as she made her back to the house. My heart skipped a beat, and I didn't know what to do, but I just screamed on top of my lungs; "mamma."

She dropped everything she was holding in her hands onto the floor, and she excitedly replied: "Mutabani wange."

The excitement we both had teleported me to the moon in a blink of an eye. My heartbeat went uncontrollably boom, and I was overcome by a type of feeling I had never felt until that sentimental moment. From the looks of how surprised my mother was, she didn't know whether to first get the broken bits of glass out of the way or to hug a lung out of me. We both smiled at each other, and I walked on the broken glass like a Goddess, and we hugged without letting go of each other. I could smell her again and felt her close like she'd been in my life for a long-time. That was the best feeling I've ever had on the day we met again. She welcomed me inside the house, and she asked me; "enjala ekuluma?"

But given I was more than excited to be around my mother, I just nodded my head because I had even forgotten how to say the simplest of words, yes. After I sat down, the next thing I was expecting her to ask me was; what I had been up to all those years, but she instead remained silent. I understand we are both quiet people who don't say much, but the silence was killing me softly. I, therefore, started a conversation by telling her what I went through to find where she lived. I also told her about the neighbour who tried playing witchy tricks on me but failed. Surprisingly before I could finish telling the story about the witch, my mother stopped me, and she asked me; "did you eat anything from that witch's house?"

"No," I answered and asked, "you seem freaked out than I was about that creepy woman; what's your story?"

She responded by telling me they were rivals because the neighbour was a sorceress, and my mother was a woman of God and good practices of humankind. We then sat down not far from each other, not knowing where to begin from or what to talk about for the fact that we hadn't seen each other for a very long time, and we both didn't know one another. I have to say before I met my mother, I always sensed a piece of the puzzle was missing in me somewhere, but I didn't know what it was precisely until when I sat close to my mother after all those years of being apart. I am telling you, I felt this was the missing piece of my puzzle connected when my heart became touched with nothing but a mother's love. I was untouchable within that moment as if I didn't have any problems. There was a decisive force in that house. And like any child around their mothers, I felt protected, and all my troubles were solved within an instant. It was as if the outside pressure and stress had dissolved into the ground before I got into the house. I was the happiest person on earth at that moment. My heart was full of joy, and I even diverted from the critical questions I had to ask. When she looked at me with this beautiful smile of hers, I decided not to ask any questions because I didn't want to sound too pushy and for her to disappear for good. She then went to her bedroom, and she returned with a big family photo album that she handed me, and she told me to go through while preparing dinner. Shortly, she joined me, and she explained pictures to picture from whom to whoever was in the photo album. We laughed at some of her photographs by how she posed, the choices of men, people's dress codes, and her facial expressions in different pictures. She had the same warm smile as mine, which lasts long after laughter. As I was going through the album, I came across a picture of a little girl and boy and asked; "who are these two angels I see in almost all of your pictures?"

She looked at me with a warm smile, and she said; "well! Those are the fruits of labour from my current marriage."

When I saw the way she spoke of them, I could see joy through her eyes, like they meant everything to her. I jealously wanted to ask her whether they were the reason she didn't look for me all those years. But on the other hand, I didn't want to ruin the good moment it was that evening. Slowly my smile started fading after discovering I wasn't the only one who stole her heart. I guess she noticed I wasn't smiley anymore, and she started reminding me of the people I hadn't seen for decades. As a mother, she noticed how fast my smile was fading, and she immediately served the food. In my culture, we have a saying; "the quickest way to re-enter someone's heart when upset is through food."

Serve them a good dish and see how happy they become. Which she did, and within a few seconds, we were right back on track. I am good at hiding my emotions and good at pretending to be happy when I'm slowly raving inside. I had many questions to ask, but that day I was about forgiving the person who went through a lot to carry me for nine months and the struggle she went through to push me out of her. We enjoyed the food she prepared and after she asked me; "Ofayo bwetugenda ffena okunonayo my fruits of labour kusomero?"

"Tewalibuzibu, tugende ffena maama." I replied.

I could see the purity of joy in my mother's eyes and how hard she struggled but didn't want to mess up with how special the moment was by asking a booklet of questions. As bad as I was tempted to, deep down, I knew I wasn't perfect, and there wasn't anything I could've done to undo the past. All I could do in my power was to embrace the present and try to grasp the delight I felt within that special moment because I didn't know what life could bring tomorrow. When we finished eating the food, I helped her to clear the dishes and later on, we went to pick up my brother and sister, who were the product of another man who wasn't my biological father. She told me he was a sweet and humble man whom she fell in love with after church services. To me, her husband seemed a bit old than she was, and he was poor as a church mouse, but who was I to judge my mother's decisions. We went together to the school where she introduced me to this sweet little girl and a humble boy aged ten and eleven. The way they were happy to see me appeared like they were told about me. We had a chat, and they told me how they were performing at school and how our mother used to talk about me all the time. They were financially struggling and lived a hard knock life, but I didn't want my curiosity to sound like derogatory remarks. And I couldn't promise to make things better without knowing exactly what was going on in their lives. My stepbrother and sister were studying barefooted, without shoes. Their uniforms had holes in them, and their packing to school was left-over from dinner the night before. They couldn't afford a tin of vaseline; they rather used leftover cooking oil to moisturize their skins before school in the morning. The four shared a bedroom, which I didn't get a chance to pep through and see how they slept. I was surprised to see how oppressed they were but somehow managed to find happiness in the little they had. I admired how they had each other and loved unconditionally. Unlike today's ungrateful generation, the children didn't have much, but they were respectful of their mother and were okay with how they lived. I looked at them with a side-eye and saw how happy they were, and I saw where my pride comes. It was all written on her face. They were experiencing something my father took away from me for decades: my consent, dignity, and joy. We had a good laugh about the silly things I used to do when little as we walked side by side, making our way back to my biological mother's house. She then decided to branch off, and we went to one of her sisters, whom we used to live with when I was still two years old, but we didn't find her home. In most East African countries, especially back home in Uganda, you don't have to book an appointment to see a family member, you just show up uninvited, and they will welcome you with open hands. I used to do that to so many of our family members back in the days when technology wasn't advanced as of today, and phones weren't abundant. My mother didn't own a phone as most ordinary people can afford. Otherwise, she could've just called her sister, but we just showed up uninvited, and we ended up being disappointed. At first, I didn't understand why she took me to see where her sister lived, but I guessed she was pointing me in the direction where I could find all the answers I was longing to hear. She mentioned I had a lovely afro that made me resemble girls. She added that some people couldn't believe I was a boy, that occasionally she had to open my pants for them to see my willy, something she found disturbing back then and couldn't say no to other than to comply. We laughed about that, too, as we made our way back home. We walked a distance of about thirty miles without feeling any muscle aches, and I didn't want the journey to end that by the time we got home, it was too late for me to head back to my boring lifestyle. I, therefore, told my mother that I would be staying at hers for the night. When we got home, I asked her to give me her sponge and water to freshen up, something she didn't find problematic. She even prepared me where to sleep on the couch. Then after that, she kept herself busy the entire time, and she didn't give me a chance to ask a billion questions I had running through my fickle brain. Have you ever been so excited to meet someone who means the world to you that your brain goes awry on the day it all happens?

Well! There was a time we sat down, and we just looked at each other instead of saying what we wanted to say to each other. She had this lasting smile that there was no room for questions by the look of how happy she was. She seemed so genuine and pure to the point that I didn't feel the need to ask questions as to why she left me behind. I just believed there must have been unlikely reasons to why the bond and love we had gone down the trench. Having tried so had to dodge the bullets all day. I guess she reached a point where she came to realise, I had unanswered questions, and she came and sat down with me for a while. I could tell she was ready to answer any questions I had on my mind. But like before, I just sat there shattered like a mutant, that not even a single word came out of the two of us. Shortly, when she came to realise, I wasn't saying anything. She went to the other room seemingly puzzled, and she attended to the little ones and her husband, who remained in the bedroom from the time he entered the house. From the looks of it, he seemed unhappy to see me, but I didn't care as long as I could spend just one night at my mother's house. I didn't want to ask questions on the first day of finding each other because I knew we had many days ahead of us to sit down and talk about our past experiences. A mistake I regret to this day. Hence, when it comes to such monumental moments, there's always a part of you that withholds information. Mine was, I just didn't know where to start from, being that I hadn't been around my mother for years, to have such a strong bond in which we could discuss openly about anything in life or smiler to the bond we had when growing up as a child. We were like strangers who had just met for the very first time. We didn't have anything in common, apart from wearing the same beautiful smile and having the same dark skin torn and looking alike. That day was the most challenging trial of life I had ever experienced. At work, I was a wordy person who spoke a salesman's language, but up to this day, I still don't know what it was precisely that silenced me not to ask my mother any questions. Yet, I came fully prepared to say whatever was on my mind, and I had even rehearsed for that day since I turned seven for my brain to zap out. I guess it's not a good mixture to be both humble and kind simultaneously. I am saying this because, when you have the two combined in one, sometimes people take you for a ride, they think you're stupid, and they forget the quieter you're, the more observant you become. The way they lived; I could tell we must've passed through a lot to reach that level of silence that not even a single conversation about the weather was coming from any of us. When she left the room, I was in; I remained puzzled with all these questions running in my head. I started blaming myself for how silly I was because I had a chance to ask all the questions I wanted to, but I somehow ceased to function. I couldn't sleep, but I'm guessing it was because I was happy to see my mom after a long decade without glancing an eye at her. She kept on checking up on me from time to time, right before I completely closed my eyes. There was one time when she stood right in the middle of the door, and she gave me a long stare with a radiant smile. I guess she was as excited as I was that day, but she didn't want to show it to me, the same way I didn't want to ask questions on the first day of us discovering one another. Her husband wasn't happy to see me, because as soon as he came back home and my cousins. Mom had all her attention on one person, me. She walked back to the bedroom, and she returned, but she seemed bothered this time around. She stepped back and forth like someone who had something to say to me, and I was the same, but none of us wanted to ruin the perfect moment we were both experiencing. I remained silent and watched her from a small window I left to peep through until I eventually fell asleep. That night I slept so peacefully, knowing my maama was watching over me. It was as if I didn't have any problems in life. For the first time in my life, I wasn't worried about anything, not even missing out on making money at work. The job I wanted to run back to was my everything because it helped develop my skill set, but spending an evening with my mom became the most fantastic heartwarming experience. When I woke up the following day, my mother told me the number of times she returned to the room and observed me as I snored myself to dreamland. She giggled and said; "singa, nabadde nekamera, nandikubye ekifananyi. Kuba wabadde so peaceful when sleeping."

"Lwendikomawo, njakuletela esimu enekusobozesa okukuba ebifananyi." I replied.

She felt the need to watch over me that night, to cover up for all the nights she missed out, to appoint where she dozed on the sofa that night. I looked at how smiley she was when talking about that night I stayed over, and I didn't want her to stop smiling. We both went silent again, and she walked back to the bedroom where the four slept on two mattresses and a worn-out fifties checkerboard throw blanket. When she walked out of their bedroom, her mood was different from when she walked in. She seemed as if she had another argument with her silent husband. You know what they say about quiet people; they're good at pretending in your face, but in reality, some are loudmouths, and others are the nastiest human beings. The following day, we all got up early for the school run. Mom prepared the four of us breakfast from the leftovers of sweet potatoes and four days expired half loaf of bread. She packed her husband's snacks in a breakfast container, and he left first, and the two of us walked out together to escort the little ones to school. On our way back from school, mom decided to accompany me to catch a taxi back to reality. We said our goodbyes, and I sadly entered the taxi heading straight to Kampala city. On sitting down quietly, I came up with a plan which was to go and make enough money so I could come back and buy her anything she didn't have, including a phone with a camera. Therefore, as soon as I got back to the real world, I worked tirelessly, and I even put in the extra effort than usual to make enough money and rescue my mother from the depressing life they lived. I also cut all expenses to achieve my goal. I was surrounded by people who praised me as a champion for selling products, but deep down, I knew myself as a coward who couldn't even ask his mom a damn question. I guess we're all masking unbearable pain.

When I was preparing to revisit: A few months later, I started buying some of the things I thought might be suitable for when I proper re-visit my biological mother. This was back in 2006 when I was young and lived a chaotic life, about twenty-two years old. I loved music more than I was afraid of women because I was timid in the company of others and didn't want anyone to get into my personal space. Even though I didn't know how to grasp life by the balls then, I was loud when it came to making money. I could sell you anything in a heartbeat, but shy to make friends. On the 26 of June 2006, I decided to go back and face my fears. So, I came to town early that day and as I was going to buy a mobile phone with a camera just the way I promised my mother. A woman in her mid-forties approached me yelling; "sebbo mukulu."

In the big crowd I was, I thought she was calling out one of the dudes behind me, and for that, I just continued minding my business, but the ignorance at that time didn't stop and neither did she stop calling me out of the crowd while pointing a finger in my direction. The comedian in me said to myself; 'damn! Do older women yell out to the younger men they have got a crush on nowadays? Funny enough, those who were around me while she was calling knew me very well at William Street in Kampala city centre. They all turned around, clapping their hands at the same time as if they were in a movie clip, and one of them screamed in delight, saying; "Ekisawe kiwedde okumwa! Genda welilile kuthente zakinamwandu."

We all had a good laugh about the situation, but it wasn't the case; she was just a messenger who came to deliver sad news to me. I walked up to her, and I jokingly said; "don't you think you are a bit older for my joystick?"

She rolled her eyes in disgust and she kissed her big gapped teeth at me, saying; "Ngakyoki kyenonya oba? Bakubajja musilver oba mugold? Tulekenawe."

What she said was provocative that I went from smiling to getting mad pissed off, and I angrily asked her with a gloomy face; "gwe ampise, nkuyambe muki nyabbo?"

"Ekikumpisiza! Onfananidde omuntu gwemanyi." She politely replied.

"Ngabanfananya abantu banji, sigweasose." I added, and I thought to myself that if she wasn't shooting her shot, then she might be a scammer of some sort.

"Maama wo ye Jenipher?" She asked.

But as soon as she mentioned my mother's names, my heart went on a straight blast and everything around me at that moment sounded like an impulsion of air through a whistle of the shofar on Rosh Hashanah, the trumpet's blast. The names caught my full attention, and I became more than interested to find out what she had on her mind. I, therefore, asked; "Maama wange wamumanyila wa?" Ye! Otegedde otya ntiyenze?"

"Nayimbanga nemaama wo mukanisa yapasita Kayiwa

eNankulabye Mengo. Nkiwa tonzijukila, naye nakulelanga ngokyalimuto." She added.

Whatever she told me, her story checked outright. In my head, I was questioning what the problem might be. But I couldn't even come any closer to guessing what exactly she wanted from me. I became thirsty and started swallowing on my own spit that nearly choked me. She saw how confused and puzzled I looked and she went straight to the point; "ononsonyiwa okukikubako kumakyagano! Naye, mbadde njagala omanyenti Maama wo yafa netumuzika emwezi ebiri gyetukubye amabega."

"Leka kulimba nawe." I energetically replied and she added; bwoba tonkakasa kankuyitile abajulizi abaliwo lwetamuzika."

She went inside the mall where she worked, and she came back with nearly the entire plaza of people who escorted my biological mother to her last home on earth. I spoke to them one by one, and they were singing the same song. She came close to where I was, and she tried hugging me, but I was all over the place. She touched my shoulder, and she said; "sandikuyimiliza kulimba kubasilina kyenfunamu."

I fainted in denial and fell flat onto the ground like a sack of potatoes, and passed out for almost an hour. I was rushed to a nearby clinic at Wilson Street, where they did everything, they could to wake me up from the shock I was in, and nothing seemed to work until a pharmacist gushed cold water on my face, and I eventually woke up. When I got up from the bench, I was still in denial because I hadn't stomached the fact that my mother was gone. She seemed healthy and energetic the first and last time I saw her. Sadly, her husband didn't have a phone to call them on and confirm whether she died and was buried like I was told. When I got off the clinic's bench, I just walked straight back to my workplace and told the guys that I wouldn't come to work for a couple of days until I confirmed my mother had passed away. The way my heart was heavy at that moment, I didn't care about anything anymore. I felt like my world had come to an end. I was mad pissed, sad and furious at the same time because my biological mother's sister knew my mobile phone number and she had enough to buy juice and inform me, but she didn't that I had to find out about my mother's death through someone who wasn't even blood-related. From that moment on, I gave up on people, and I just didn't care about anyone anymore. My mind was deluded into thinking if I got close to people, they would also die like my mother. Again, I didn't know the way to the place where they buried my biological mother. And for the second time, I had to pass through someone I didn't want to ever glance an eye at. I had to choose between hating my mother's sister or going there for help one last time. This was harder than a woman's struggle to choose through her closet for which dress to wear for a dinner date. The world felt so small that I wished the soil swallowed me or something from outer space vanished me from the eyes of the earth. And from that moment on, I could feel how painful it is to lose a mother or a loved one. Before, people spoke of death, and I couldn't understand what it actually meant until it knocked on my doorstep. I stayed in bed for as long as I can remember. I didn't care about showering or even getting up to cook something to eat. I switched off my mobile phone and locked myself inside the house for a month without talking to anyone to appoint where my landlord knocked on my door thinking I was dead or something terrible had happened to me. My biological mother's sudden death wasn't unfair at all. The most painful thing that kept on playing in my head was that we had just reconnected with my mom, then she had the nerve to leave. She left me in the total darkness of pain. Suppose you are someone who doesn't care about your parents or the one who is unbothered to help them through their struggles. Man, you must be the saddest creature on earth.. Do you think your life is hard now because your ventures aren't skyrocketing? Wait until you lose someone you love dearly or the parents who sacrificed almost everything, they had for you to be what you are today. Then, you will understand how hard the holidays, birthdays and graduations celebration or when you achieve a new goal that deserves the presence of a constant absent parent, but they can't be there to share the laughter. Whilst shutting down from the outside world inside a pitch-dark room, I stayed for months. I thought about committing suicide over and over again repeatedly. I can't even count the number of times I carelessly crossed the road to be taken on a sport. I became fed up with waking up every morning to the pain of knowing she was not coming back. I started blaming myself for not being there through her struggles, not making enough effort to be there on her deathbed and having missed her burial.

On second thought, I couldn't blame myself much because no one from my mother's side informed me that she was sick. But still, I felt like it was my obligation to go back on time; maybe I would have been her saviour for life. Perhaps she would've told me how she felt and apologised for missing my birthdays and being in each other's life. Most definitely could have told me what went wrong with my father, whom I couldn't ask a thing because we weren't talking to each other by then. I was so mad at him for separating me from my mother. Nevertheless, as upsetting as the situation was, I knew it wasn't in my place to hate because I am not someone who holds grudges for so long. Therefore, for the kind heart, I am, I forgave my father in the end because he might've done what he thought was the right thing to do. Besides, who was I to judge another when I am not perfect either. According to what I went through as a separated child, it's not the wisest move to separate a child from their parents, let it be from their mother or father. During those thirty-four most difficult days I spent in my room, deep down, I knew forgiveness was a must; otherwise, if I weren't so careful, I would've become the same person who hurt me. I didn't have a strong bond with my father, given that when I was a child, the only time we talked was when I was in the wrong. So, I became so stubborn for him to punish me as much as he could to a point where I thought he might as well drive me back to my biological mother. My father isn't an emotional person. He was the kind of person who could repeatedly smack me and move on with his life that very moment. I felt like my father was too angry with me that to this day, I have never sat down to ask him how he felt each time I asked about visiting my mother or why he was so tough on me. While I was in a pitch-dark room, I thought about so many things trying to make sense of things, but none of what I thought of made sense. The courage it took me to get out of bed every morning after hearing about my birth mother's death to face the same trauma over and over again was enormous. I prayed, Allah to give my mother a second chance and bring her back to life. Trust me; if it were to happen, I would have traded everything I had to have one extensive conversation with her about what went wrong. But unfortunately, life doesn't work like that, and you don't often get second chances. Besides praying on it, the librarian I was dating before I went on the adventure to find my mother crossed my mind. When I thought about the number of times, I asked her out, while she came up with excuse after excuse; "I am not really up to dating at the moment because I have university to focus on, and I am trying to balance having a life doing my course work."

I became more heartbroken. The pain of rejection felt like that of a fresh wound stabbed twice. Even though my heart was all over the place, deep down, I truly adored the librarian because, during my challenging moments, she was the only person who genuinely cared about how I felt or how my miserable day went. I always passed by her workplace to mine, and on the days, I didn't show up, she could come by to see if I was doing ok. I told her about almost everything that was going on in my life. Still, I somehow forgot to tell her about my mother's death because I wasn't thinking straight on the day I found out about my mother's passing, and given that, I returned home early, and she spent all day at the university. Of which I didn't want to leave the house. I didn't care anymore and wasn't interested in talking to anyone those days I was grieving. Days added up without stepping a foot out of the house, and I suppose she might've wondered why I wasn't showing up to her workplace anymore. Surprisingly, on my twenty-fifth day of grieving the death of mom. The Librarian found out where I lived, and I heard on knock on the door. 'Puff, puff.' When I withstood opening the door, she angrily said; "I know you're in there because I have just spoken to your concerned neighbours who've been wondering what happened to you."

She sat at the footstep of my door while talking me into giving in, but that wasn't enough effort to get me out of my bed or the house. She knocked for almost an hour nonstop, and I was still not bothered. She then added; "if I am to lose my job or miss out on lectures today, so be it. But I am not going anywhere until you open this door."

She persistently knocked on the door until she made a big scene to arouse my neighbour's attention, they came out of their houses to see what was going on. She managed to call the landlord to open the door, the info she failed to mention that he was involved in my mess. Thus, before I knew it, the door was wide open. The librarian walked right in with the caring neighbours, and the house was a total mess of darkness. Once the good neighbours confirmed I was alive, they seemed relieved, and they all went back to whatever it was they were doing. She pulled the blanket off me, and she said; "get out of bed and have a shower, stinker, then after you will tell me what's going on with you."

"I'm not getting out of bed simply because there's nothing to tell," I replied and covered myself again.

The librarian didn't add anything to the words that came out of my mouth. She just walked off silently, and she returned a few seconds later with an ice-cold jug of water she poured on me while asking; "how about now, stinker?"

I jumped out of bed as if the house was catching fire,

screaming on top of my lungs; "Oi! Why did you do that for?"

She just stood there enjoying the show. I walked away feeling upset. However, even though she poured a cold jar of water on me in bed. But to be honest, seeing the librarian somehow made me feel better. I took my time in the shower reflecting on my life and how to approach my Later mother's sister to direct me to Masulita, where they buried my mother. I was so upset with all her family members that if I went to see them the day I found out about mom's death, they never bothered to look for me. I probably would've made a scene about it or even ended in jail. Who knows what might've happened? Those days I locked myself in a darkroom during my mental breakdown helped me discover that a grieving person's best conversations are those they have by themselves. Even though my thoughts were rusty, I had the room to myself without being disrupted by the outside world or interrupted by technology. I have grieved in my own way that has helped me to reflect on my life. I learned the hard way that self-control is the best strength the heartbroken can have. Calmness is a mastery; a very few people naturally possess. I fought my thoughts to get to that point where my mood doesn't shift based on what was going on in my life or what my mother's immediate family did for not calling me to at least be there to hear her last words. I also learnt not to allow my current situation to control my life, and from that moment on, I refused to let my emotions overpower my intelligence. It wasn't as easy as it may sound when you talk about it. I had to work repeatedly hard to overcome all obstacles that were hindering me from stepping out of the house since I heard about the death of my beloved biological mother. When the librarian came by, her presence somehow gave me the strength I needed to get back on track before death took something valuable from me. I spent three hours in the bathroom discussing what to say to my late mother's sister before asking for directions to their family graveyard. I honestly didn't know where to start from because I was so upset with my mother's entire family, especially her. My mind went on a milestone of thoughts that by the time I returned to my house, the librarian had already cleaned my house, and she had cooked me something to eat too. I quickly changed, and as soon as I sat down to eat, my first question was; "last time we talked, you were busy with university and work combined. So, tell me! What made you change your mind?"

"Life has a way of turning tables, Mr." She replied.

"If that isn't the truth, then, I don't know what it is?" I added.

I had a quick forced laugh, and slowly my smile started fading, then tears followed. When I became emotional, the Librarian handed me a white handkerchief, and she said; "come on, go ahead and cry it out. Whatever it is will come to an end."

"This won't be over anytime soon. This scar is forever, and it's right on my heart." I replied, whipping like a three-year-old.

"Ok! I am utterly perplexed. You never mentioned you're suffering from heart conditions. Can you please explain more before I run out of my mind? I am starting to fall for your type, and when I didn't see you for a whole damn month. Tell you what? I had a dream last night when you were being chased by angry snakes and thought you must be facing real-life difficulties. I cancelled my lectures and called in sick for work today, plus it took me a lot of guts to find out where you live. You are a hard man to find because no one knows where you live, but in my feminine way, I found you." She added.

"Hey! Relax. My situation has nothing to do with anything you have mentioned. I was informed about a month ago that my mother passed away, and I didn't get the chance to hear her last words or even bury her." I replied.

She looked at me with a saddened face, and she said; "Oh no! I am so sorry to hear about your mother's passing."

"You don't need to apologise. It's not your fault." I responded.

"Is there anything I can do to help or make you feel better?" She asked.

"I appreciate your concern, but at this time. There's nothing anyone can do to bring back someone from the dead or even change the way I feel." I added, and we both went silent for a while.

The breakfast she cooked was Ugandan green bananas boiled together with goat's guts and red grounded peanuts. The food smelt delicious, but I didn't have the appetite to eat anything. Not because I didn't like what she cooked, but because I wanted to starve myself to death. Ever since I discovered my mother's death, I honestly felt like there wasn't anything left for me and for that, I didn't have a purpose of living. She encouraged me to eat, and it wasn't easy for me. The appetite I had before death knocked on my front door was among the precious things I lost in the pain of grieving. I despised every day I lived that I wished the lord could take me and re-join my mother wherever she took off too. To break the silence between us, she asked me; "have you thought about finding out whether your mother died? Think about it! What if the person who told you lied?"

"Yes, I have thought about it. But the thing is, I don't even know how to get to where she was buried." I replied.

"Are you telling me, no one in your family knows where your mother was buried, not even your father?" The librarian asked.

"None of those I grew up with knew where the place was, not even my father. We never spoke about my mother in the house where I grew up. To appoint where most people believed the person who raised me was the biological mother, that up to this day, those who didn't hear about my birth mother's passing or that she ever existed can't be convinced she wasn't my birth mother. I can't blame them because my second special mother treated me like her own without socialism, and I am forever grateful. Maybe it was because we never told anyone, and we never gave them a reason to doubt us." I added.

"So, how did you find out about your mother's death?" She curiously asked.

"The person who told me about my mother's death was a woman. I didn't even get a chance to ask for her name, contact details, or shop number. The thing is, I couldn't think straight because I was in tremendous shock." I honestly replied.

"That's sad, man." She added, and we both went silent for

a moment. Then I told her the story of how it all happened. That by the time I finished telling my sad story, the librarian didn't want to leave me by myself.

She, later on, wore one of my short pants and my blue shirt that had the map of the United States, and she washed the blue she had on earlier on. Be wilding; I was a shy and old-fashioned person whenever it came to matters of talking to women. This was a subject I didn't have much interest in back then, not because I despised them or anything along those lines, but because my goal was to make enough money not to cry to my parents for help. I remember many female customers made passes at me, and I had never brought any of them to my house before. So, we both looked at each other awkwardly, wondering what was coming up next. We laid down and came up with all these plans on approaching my late mother's sister and how she could be of use. Before I was the type of person who never made plans for anything, not even note-taking, and I have kept that attitude to this day. If I want something done, I get it done there and then, period. That as soon as a plan pops up in my head, I immediately go and work on it. Shortly, the librarian kissed me on my lips, and I remember blowing it up by telling her; "we can't do anything out of the ordinary tonight. Please don't get me wrong. It's not that I am not looking forward to giving you some of the goodies I possess. I also have feelings for you, and for that specific reason, I want our first day to be unforgettable, plus I don't want you to feel as if you're taking advantage of me because I am in a helpless state of mind."

"Boy don't flatter yourself! Who told you something was going to happen? You won't get this 'Kuki' of mine in that state of mind you are in right now. I want you to have it when it's the only thing you can think of." She jokingly added, and we cuddled until we snored in each other's face.

However, I have to say; having someone besides you when you're going through a wrecking moment somehow rejuvenates your soul. The family members I grew up with seemed distanced as we both lived on a different planet from each other. I hadn't told my immediate family about the bad news for a month. I just didn't know where to start, and I didn't know whether confronting my mother's side of the family would upset them more than their ignorance did to me. Of which, I always felt like he totally gave up on my mother, but not informing him would've made me look as bad as my mother's sister, who knew my number but didn't even bother texting me about my mother's conditions. We slept in the same room that night, and nothing happened. Not that I wasn't capable, but because I wasn't myself or in the right state of mind to a point where I didn't even give a damn whether she thought of it as a weakness for not trying to ask for some. My mind was all over the place to ask the Librarian for sex in the middle of the night. I had a huge crush on her, but not on that day with how bad things were for me. The next day the Librarian sneaked out before I woke up, that by the time I opened my eyes, she had already left the house. I got up feeling much better than I was for the past month and travelled back to my mother's sister's place. When I got there, I didn't ask her about how my mother died until I saw her grave with my own eyes because I hadn't registered it yet that my mother was gone. At a certain point, I thought I was going crazy when I thought she might've gone somewhere and buried the wrong body.

Cultural wise, Buganda makes up almost 80% of Ugandan's population; most Baganda people cry each time they see a family member who looks like a loved one who passed away. And in this case, I was that family member who resembled my mom. Consequently, what shocked me was my mother's sister, who didn't seem to show any emotional reaction about her sister's passing. She was so happy like the last time we met. She didn't even question how I felt about losing my mother. However, she seemed as if she was waiting for me to come by her place so she could take me to Masulita, where their place of burial was. With the questions I had in mind, I wanted to ask her about how my mother died, but I somehow froze and started talking to myself instead; what if I ask questions right now and I don't get a chance to know where she was buried? Uganda is the motherland and the pearl of Africa, where most of its parts are still keeping the margin with its modernity. Every household has its family-owned graveyard, unlike developed countries where they bury everyone in the same cemetery, like farmers planting sessional seeds on the same farm from January to December. These graveyards aren't an area a stranger can just dig up to salt and fire up the deceased's body like it's done in Supernatural. The spirits will hunt you down like someone who lives in a haunted house. My late mother's sister looked at me and she said; "bulijo netegeka ngankusubila okujja tugende olambule kumaka ga Maamawo amagya."

"Nganange ndimukubo nzijja." I replied and she added; "nga byebigere binobyendaba."

Deep down, I was boiling mad because I gave her my number to reach out in case of anything, but she didn't even text to inform me about my mother's funeral. I sensed there must've been a reason why I wasn't told about my mother's passing by any of her family members. I held onto my thoughts not to ask questions that could've ruined the moment, and I decided to swallow my pride and went with the flow. I forced myself to keep calm, but words were raving right at the back of my throat like that of a madwoman. My vocal fold became overly loaded like a broken pipe covered with a plastic bag to prevent a flood, but that was also about to burst any minute soon. While at my late mother's sister's place, I didn't sit for long because she had everything, she wanted for the road prepared. She handed me one of her bags, and we took off. The good thing was I came prepared for whatever decision she made. We boarded a taxi to Old Kampala taxi park, and we walked to the new taxi park where we boarded a taxi to Masulita. When we reached the journey halfway, she walked me through buying a few things like ten kilos of sugar, a loaf of bread, a three-litre Jerrycan of cooking oil, four bars of soap, and we had something to eat in a local restaurant. When we reached halfway through the journey, the driver made a quick stopover in a small town to stretch his legs and for everyone on board to get something to eat. We momentarily continued with the journey, and as we were approaching our final destination. I got a weird feeling that gave me goosebumps all over my body, and within ten minutes of that, I could feel my mother's energy around like an invisible shield protecting me. That before we reached the place where my late mother was laid to sleep, the baffling feeling I had already convinced me my mother was among the people laid in the family graveyard. And as puzzling as it may sound, I couldn't exemplify how mutual I was feeling to mom's sister, so I kept that to myself not to seem like I was going out of my mind. When we reached the house where my late mother and all her sisters were born, we entered inside the un-cemented brick house. We greeted another sister to my late mother. The sister I came with introduced me to the person who was responsible for taking care of the graveyard located twenty feet at the back of the house, literally in the middle of a healthy garden. The sister we found at home knew me, but I didn't know who she was. It was easy to tell because I looked exactly like my late mother.

"Olinga ekifananyi kya maama wo. Kale wafanana oli nokamala. Guno omusayi gusika." She spoke and she also mentioned that she last saw me when my late mother ran off to Kampala with my father years back and never saw me again until that day. Usually, village people cook big meals for their visitors, but this time she didn't cook anything because she wasn't informed, I was coming and she didn't have a single penny because her big sister hadn't sent her any upkeep.

"Nga nsanyuse okubalaba. Naye munansonyiwa obutabafumbila kakulyakoma. Ebikozesebwa bwampedeko." The family graveyard keeper welcomed us again.

"Nange nsanyuse okukulaba, nyabo." I responded and she added; "Naye munansonyiwa obutabategekera kyakulya wadde."

"Tewalibuzibu. Twafunye ekyokulya ngatenajawano." I added.

"Eeeeeee! Vawonawe. Nze olwonemunelabila? Mulibazibu." She sadly added.

"Tetusobola kwelabila. Mutabani, wo yakwetigidde, etu

mumugugugwe." Her sister replied while we unpacked the valuables, we came with on our way.

The two sisters caught up, and we were served tea. Shortly, I asked to be directed where the graveyard was, and one of the sisters didn't hesitate to escort me because I was too afraid to go there by myself, that even if you were to win a bet of a million Ugandan shillings or pounds. I honestly wouldn't bother participating, but when I reached the graveyard, I was like superman. I kind of felt at home, at ease and connected with the aura. She explained who those people were, and most of them were their deceased sisters, grandchildren and the two grandparents I once lived with as a child. Whilst walking through the cemetery, I remembered the last meal mom cooked me last time I saw her, though I was too young to acknowledge she was dying at the time. She always had a smile on her face, but she was the most brutal human being I've ever come across. She was very strict and took no bulls or crap of any kind. Looking around, almost the entire graveyard was falling apart, and some plots, especially my mom's, had three deep holes in them that could keep the dead hydrated for a decade. The number was big of those laid to rest in that place, but only my late mother's parents were adequately built in the '80s, where their houses only needed to be refurbished. When the person I came with saw how generous I was after buying a few eatables of stuff for those in the village, she thought I was fully loaded. They must have thought, living abroad, I pick money off trees. She therefore, said; "yengakikoze bulungi nojja. Ate banaffe tebafunye mukisa. Nanti, bona bagenda kuzimbwa."

"Sente ezinagenda wano ngasizilina, mukaddewange." I

politely replied.

She gave me a wicked long stare, and she negligibly laughed like it was a joke for me to say that, but little did she know I was in between jobs. I lightly grinned, not to seem disrespectful because deep down, I knew how deep my pockets could go. Besides, it wasn't going to be done that day we visited. I sat down on my mother's grave in tears while counting how much I was going to spend in that place. They tried confronting me, and the more they did, the more they made it worse. I started feeling upset to hear them speak, and I kindly asked them to leave me alone for a few minutes before saying something inappropriate to hurt their feelings. Among the important lessons I've learnt in life is that self-care is not arguing with wonky people who are usually committed to proving you wrong or misunderstanding your point of view. I started asking my mom's grave; "why did you have to leave so soon? We had just met, and things were going to be different. Why didn't you wait for me to come back for a second visit? What went wrong? You seemed happy and healthy to die suddenly, but why this time."

What is meant by grief?: Grief painfully hurts people in complex ways, and everyone grieves in their way when they lose someone they love dearly. I continued talking to myself back and forth in tears and as I was still there sat in the middle of the graveyard, crying my eyes out. A mighty wailing wind blew past me, and that freaked a life out of me, but I somehow felt strong and determined to face whatever was to come out of a howling wind.

A few minutes later, a brown coloured, red-faced Cisticola erythrops bird, Ugandans nicknamed 'nkazalujja' flew from where the wind blew from, and it stood only on mom's grave for about twenty minutes, scrutinising right at me. That gave me goosebumps and enough vindication to fully digest the fact that she wasn't coming back. Shortly, the little bird flew away like Peter, heading towards the direction of the wind. I emotionally got up in tears and started plucking blades of grass off my mother's grave. From that moment on, I honestly don't know how I managed to pull it off because I cleared all graves by hand that by the time the two sisters returned with tools, the place was grass-free, fresh and ready for the final touches. The two were utterly shocked to find the place an inch-perfect. They looked at me supposedly, and they asked at the same time; "who the heck are you?"

Everything I did and the way I felt while grieving the loss of my mom were all extraordinarily out of the ordinary because I don't know where the level of energy I had whilst sitting in the middle of the graveyard came from, and neither did I know how energetic grief was until when I put all my strength into plucking grass off all graves. It painfully hurts to lose a parent, but it's even more painful when you don't get a chance to say goodbye, hear their last words or when you are not able to be there for them on their last days before their departure. It's like being stabbed in the chest with a knife and swirling it round to make you feel that sensational sharp stinging pain as the knife reps off meat down to your bone. The greatest mistake I made was to think I had enough time to revisit my mom. Meeting her was a stroke of luck that I never thought would have happened if I continued procrastinating to go on an adventure to find out where she lived. I have learnt a valuable lesson not to take things lightly and valuables for granted. Hug your loved ones if you must and let go of any anger you hold towards them. Forgive them and show them that you care and love them regardless because tomorrow is never promised, and you can't predict what happens next. Appreciate good people around you and the little they contribute to your soul because you might not have any of it tomorrow. If you still have both parents, classify yourself among the few lucky ones. Show them how much you love them and appreciate the sacrifices they made for you to be here today. If they made mistakes, it's because they are human beings, just like you and me. Make sure you forgive them if you feel they mistreated you as a child, and let go of what was in the past. Remember, parents, are never wrong because whatever they do, they do it in the interest of their children. Becoming a parent, you get to understand what your parents went through. You are lucky you got an education, and you maybe work underneath an AC and a coffee shop around the corner, but they didn't have that because they wanted you to have everything they didn't have or couldn't afford in life. And if it weren't for their contributions towards your upbringing, you wouldn't have existed. For parents out there, whatever happens between you two grownups shouldn't evolve around children or have to hurt children involved in your relationship. Your children aren't to be blamed for the things that go wrong in your relationship. Remember, you made them out of love, and they became the results of what you called love in the beginning. Consequently, their presence should represent the good times you two shared when deepened in a fetish love affair.

Speaking from experience as a child who grew up without

the other parent, it is hard for the children. Let bygones be, put your ego aside and let your children see their other parent. Deal with your issues the other way and let your children out of useless deadbeats play. When your children grow up and refuse to look after you when ageing, please don't blame them; blame your actions towards their father or mother you mistreated in their presence. Some people don't care about their parents or even support your needs or can't they even buy you a house or build you one. And for those who can't forgive their parents or can't even associate with their parents because of what they did years ago. To those out there who think having money or owning the most expensive things makes you exemplary than someone who went through a tun of pain to carry you for nine bloody months and pushed you out of her flower to anoint of losing her life, you are miserable than a church mouse. No matter how damaged or poorly hurt you are. Forgiveness is the first step to naturing yourself and one of the most excellent remedies for healing a broken heart. I have also learnt that when you forgive someone who wrongs you. You don't necessarily do it for them; it's rather for your own benefit. Therefore, doing so liberates you from mental suffering, not for the sake of the friendship, but for your own good. Having sat right in the middle of the graveyard for a few hours, I acknowledged that if I continued to be upset with my mom's sisters. I will only be wasting my breath. I, therefore, forgave her, and we moved on. We sat down, and we started making plans on how we were going to finalise the graveyard. We calculated the number of cement bags, bricks, and sand to use. Luckily enough, someone rented half of their land to make sand bricks. She called, and we agreed on the number of bricks to buy from him. When all material was agreed upon, my mother's sister suggested we go and sleepover at their elder brother's house, which was fifteen minutes away from the house where they grew up. I paid for all material cash in hand, and we rode a Boda, Boda, to their elder brother. Ugandans are known for their kindness and generosity, to a point where you don't necessarily need to book an appointment to visit a family member. You just show up, and they will prepare you something to eat. Thus, when we got there my mother's sister asked; "Mutebbe ani Ono Gwenzizenaye?"

And without having to squint an eye to see who I was, they immediately replied; "Ono mutabani wamwanyoko omugenzi."

Her brother walked to me with open arms and he hugged a lung out of me, saying; "kale wafanana maama wo nokamala."

We had a good laugh about it as he held his hand onto my shoulders, and he walked me inside the house. As all villagers do, we came in the middle of having dinner around six pm. Like I mentioned earlier, with our people, there's no need to book an appointment like it is here it is in Utopia. Thus, there was enough food for almost three people, which they served us without complaining it wasn't enough. Dinning in Uganda is slightly different, unlike in Utopia. We all sat down on locally sewed mats in a circle big enough to cover the entire family, and we dug in until everyone was certified. They bonded as any family would, and I slightly felt like an outsider because I honestly didn't know where to start from, and I didn't have anything to say. Their brother kept on coming up with a batch of stories from the past I didn't know anything about. And wherever they said something amusing, they all laughed, looking my way, waiting to see my reaction, and I was just there smiling like any fool would find themselves caught up in the middle of a conversation they have no hint about. They somehow managed to involve me not to feel left out. Time passed as they went on and on about specific things they hadn't talked about for a very long time. Their brother kept on thanking me for bringing her sister to visit. He mentioned that he knew she was always coming to their town, but she never stopped by his house. I just sat there smilingly, deeming like a bridge connecting them all. When we finished eating, my uncle's wife prepared me a one-inch mattress and beddings to sleep on one side of the front room and my mom's sister on the right-hand side. My uncle's family stayed with us in the sitting room, and they continued to talk until we were all worn out. I woke up early the following day and informed my uncle that I had to go back to the city to meet some notable clients, and for that reason, I couldn't stay for breakfast. She handed me the budget, and I left to go and make enough money to come back to Masulita, Uganda and complete the graves. I looked at how much I had to spend while going to town and wanted to work only on my mom's grave. I quickly rang mom's sister and informed her that I might not be able to afford the quoted money, and she told; "it's a curse to work on one tomb in our culture."

"How so?" I asked.

"That alone leads to the death of all family members. As it causes the dead to feel left out." She added.

She told me that I had to work at least on three graves or all of them, but I couldn't work only on my mother's grave. Thus, I had no choice other than to work on all of them. I cut down on my expenditure for me to be able to keep up with the budget at hand, and I worked tirelessly to save for the project. But unexpected circumstances tend to happen whenever you're endeavouring to accomplish something. As I was starving myself not to overspend, I seldom found it hard to get to work that I lost my customers base to the Indian retailer who came up with cheap home appliances made from China. Who doesn't like to buy affordable products?

I, therefore, had to change course and enter the music industry. I began promoting upcoming musicians in my own way. At the same time, as installing music in people's mobile phones, iPods, MP3 players, and burnt CDs, I was editing videos and had a video production company, namely; Zac Entertainment. It wasn't easy convincing my customers to support me in this one. Thus, it, therefore, wasn't easy because even the musicians I promoted weren't paying a single penny because they were also upcoming. Still, they promised to recommend customers to me, which some did. It wasn't easy during the first periods of my carrier. As any man starting a new business would struggle to stand on their two feet, so did I struggle to allocate funds to keep the business running, and convincing customers to move from their service providers seemed almost impossible. The Indian man who took me out of business called me several times, asking me to join hands and work for him, and I refused. I honestly can't stress enough about the number of times I went on lockdown just because I couldn't afford to pay up the rent. And on the days, I managed to borrow money from friends to keep the doors open. Those were the days' customers barely showed up to support my journey. It was like a roller coaster of problems attached to a ghost train in supernatural. The Indian businessman who wanted me to work for him often sent spies to find out whether I was successful or not, and none of that took me off my course. However, there were times I sat down after paying Allah to save me from drowning and thought of giving up trying and going to work for the Indian man. Then a few customers showed up, which positively geared me not to give up the fight. Sometimes customers came to my shop to support me, and there were months when I couldn't make a single penny. My business became less like a roller coaster of problems. As life continued tasting my patience, so did my landlord add pressure on top of what was oppressing me. The landlord locked us down on multiple occasions because we couldn't afford the rent. Sometimes the shop could take three months while locked, and on top of that, I had to pay the rent for the months our shops were locked down.

Come what may, I had to make a living to stay in the game, I, therefore, emailed all my customers and asked them to call me directly if they required my services, and they agreed. Those concerned asked why the shop was on lockdown, and I honestly explained that I couldn't afford to pay for months I didn't use, but all they cared for as their monies paid in full. Usually, problems pile up when you're facing your hardest times. The timeline I gave the family members I promised to help with building the graveyard passed, and they started calling me while I kept on ignoring their calls because I didn't have the precise words to describe the situation I was undergoing through. Nevertheless, with everything I was undergoing, little did I grasp my struggles were moulding me into a much more robust person. The most horrific experience I have ever encountered was the sudden death of my mother. I have never been tested like it was when I was mourning mom's death because obstacles started befalling all at the same time as if I was being scolded by life. I respired in regrets as I toiled tirelessly to make enough money to work on the unfinished graveyard. One month after the deadline passed, I started having uncanny wet dreams about a faceless little girl who was suffocating underwater, and I thought to myself maybe it was because I was under a lot of stress. Then, a week passed without having any more of those weird wet dreams, and I thought that was it, but then that was followed by a different form of wet dreams about a faceless woman who was drowning as she was asking me to save her. At first, I didn't understand what these dreams meant exactly. Thinking about it, what that meant was that water was entering inside my late mom's grave. The cemetery builder mom's sister hired to cement her grave on the day of her burial didn't do a proper job because little animals dug multiple holes within the sides of the grave, which enabled pouring rain to fill her up with water inside. So, me having these apparitions in my dreams was my mom's way of crying for help, and for that, I knew I had to wear my big boy pants and own up to my end of the bargain. There were days I thought to myself; "how can someone be here one-minute breathing and cease to exist the next?"

The Grieving Process: When your parent dies in your adulthood, there is almost an unspoken expectation that it will not hit you head-on. An adult is expected to accept death as a part of life, to handle all sudden losses in an appropriate adult manner. But really, what does that mean? That you should not be sad? That you should be so grateful they didn't die when you were a child that you don't need to mourn your parent? Such considerations demonstrate an under-estimation of grief. Grief is the reflection of the connection that has been lost. That loss does not diminish because you are an adult or because your parent lived a long life. Our society places enormous pressure on us to get over the loss, to get through the grief. But how long do you grieve for a man who was your father for 20 years? Do you grieve less for your mother of 30 years? The loss happens in a moment, but its aftermath lasts a lifetime. The grief is real because loss is real. Each loss has its own imprint, as distinctive and unique as the person we lost. It doesn't matter how old we are. When we lose an aged parent, many times well-intentioned friends try to offer condolences, such as, "He had a long life, you must be happy about that," or, "You're so lucky he died so quickly."

However, these words often do not resonate as we suffer the loss of a father or mother who had been by our side our entire life. We will never have another father. We will never have another mother. Every grieving process you are going through is a natural response to loss. It's the emotional suffering you feel when someone you love is dead, and you know they are not returning to life. Often, the pain of loss can feel overwhelming. You experience all kinds of difficult and unexpected emotions, from shock or anger to disbelief, guilt, and profound sadness. The pain of grief also disrupts your physical health, making it difficult to sleep most of the time, loss of appetite, and sometimes you don't think straight. These are normal reactions to loss, and the more significant the loss, the more intense your grief will be. Coping with the loss of someone you love is one of life's most extensive and trickiest challenges. On the other hand, everyone experiences grief differently. For someone who has lost a parent, the pain of loss won't be the same as for someone who has lost a job that's easily replaced or someone who wasn't detached from their being. Many people who have lost a loved one experience grief in various episodes of grieving the loss of a loved one. When you lose a close loved one, you go through commonalities and distinct stages, such as denial, fury, and depression. There are a few more to name, but you may not know that these stages aren't about the grief of someone dying but rather something extremely different. When grieving the loss of a parent, you will have loads of questions running through your head like I was; "this my fault? Was I supposed to feel this way? Why am I the one to carry this burden? How am I supposed to feel at this point? Is it wrong for me to feel a certain way when others feel different?"

Whatever your loss, it's personal to you and you only. No one will ever understand your pain better than you. So please don't feel ashamed about how you think or believe it's only appropriate to grieve for a certain period of time. If the person, pet, relationship, or situation is/was vital to you, it's natural to mourn the loss you are experiencing for as long as it takes you to. Whatever the cause of your grief, though, there are healthy ways to cope with the pain that, in time, can ease your sadness and help you come to terms with your loss, find a new meaning to life, and eventually move on with your life. The key to restoration is understanding where you are in the grief process and what you're willing to do to overcome the pain you're experiencing. But it all starts with acceptance and self-care. Grief is experienced in different forms that depend upon how strong one's mentality is, emotional state, and events of occurrence. When death ripped the other half away from me, I was able to recover without therapy because I was more robust than the pain itself. However, suppose death was to rip from someone emotionally unstable, also known as a borderline personality disorder, a mental illness characterised by a long-term pattern of unstable relationships, distorted sense of self, and intense emotional reactions. In that case, this person is more likely to engage in self-harm and other dangerous behaviour such as attempting suicide. The grieving experience is different for everyone, and so are the days of experiencing painful moments. When you're grieving, there will be days where you will wake up feeling strong to face the world or feeling unstoppable like you can handle any obstacles. There will be days where you will wake up feeling like you've been hit by a truck that you won't be bothered to get out of bed to make a bloody sandwich. If I remember correctly, there were days I wasn't even bothered to get up for a pee. I had a green bucket right next to my bed, in which I eased myself because I wasn't bothered to speak with my neighbours. I went through all these grieving episodes to help me notice what I was ignoring. I gradually accepted life's ups and downs and learned to uplift myself through this wonderful journey. Emotions ranged from anger to sadness or even numbness. You will be tasted in so many ways, and these grieving episodes will make you feel like a fragile glass that, at a certain point, you won't be bothered to face the reality of things. Consequently, I want you to remember these grieving episodes like a willy; sometimes it's up, and sometimes it's down, but it doesn't stay hard forever.

Everything you feel is valid, and despite how intense your emotions may run wield, you're most likely experiencing the episodes of grief such as:

- ✓ **Denial:** "This can't be happening to me."
- ✓ **Anger:** "Why is this happening? Who is to blame?"
- ✓ **Bargaining:** "Make this not happen, and in return, I will change I promise."
- ✓ **Depression:** "I am too sad to do anything."
- ✓ **Acceptance:** "I am at peace with what happened."

When you're experiencing any of the mentioned emotions of grief, it may help to know that your reaction is natural and that you will heal in time. However, not everyone who goes through these emotional stages heals the same way, and that's okay. Contrary to popular belief, you don't have to go through each step to heal because everyone's healing process is different from everyone else's. In fact, some people resolve their grief without going through any of these stages and they don't seek therapy either, because our grieving has a different meaning attached to it and we are mentally built differently. Nevertheless, if you happen to go through any of the grieving steps as mentioned in this piece of writing, chances are; you might not experience them in neat, sequential order. So don't panic, freak out or even worry about what you should be feeling or which stage you are supposed to be in. When I lost my mother, I didn't seek therapy because I felt I didn't need to. I knew I was strong enough to fight on my own, even though I went through three stages:

- ✓ **Denial:** This can't be happening, we've just met?"
- ✓ **Anger:** Why did you have to take my mother of all the people in this world? My late mother's family members are to blame."
- ✓ **Acceptance:** Now, I'm at peace with what happened.

Reaching acceptance didn't happen overnight because I passed through hellfire gates to reach the acceptance stage. Some people move through each phase of grief on their own as I did, whereas others may need the help of a shrink. Mind you, I was still the same tearful person I was from the first day I heard my mother's death. The heavy burden of pain in my chest was difficult to bear. Grief can be debilitating for those dealing with heavy losses, and there's the possibility of developing mental health disorders. No matter the sorrow, grief is a universal experience. It's not a matter of whether you'll grieve, but when? Many have sought help for their grief, and those who have sought guidance have responded positively. Some people are natural-born fighters like myself; we just rebuild ourselves from what we do every day. That doesn't mean the strong ones are exempt from pain, or they have metallic hearts that don't allow them to feel pain. Grief is a strange beast that we learn to live with. We don't get over it as if it were a surmountable object. We can become more comfortable with our discomfort but there is no finite time for grief as there is no finite time for love. Grief is often a private affair that others cannot share or perhaps even understand. Grief can spring out of drawers and cupboards, off shelves, from photographs, wafts to our nostrils upon a perfume, is precipitated by music, clutches at our heart, hollows out our insides and plummets us to the depths. It is indeed a strange beast to know and understand, to embrace, digest and assimilate. You may well wonder what exactly is meant by a grief trigger. This is anything that brings up memories of a loss that has happened to you. The stronger your demeanour is the higher the chances are to fight. They are also human like you and me who might as well be questioning grief; what should you expect? What is normal to experience during grief? What may seem like a developing or underlying problem that needs help?

Common grief reactions include difficult feelings, thoughts, physical sensations, behaviours and feelings. People like us who have experienced loss may have a range of feelings. This could include shock, numbness, sadness, denial, despair, anxiety, anger, guilt, loneliness, depression, helplessness, relief, and yearning. But there are other triggers that can also trip you up unexpectedly. Like times when you see someone who looks like your loved one or hear of someone with the same name or age or job. Favourite colours, songs, TV shows, food – all of these links can cause a memory to ignite some feelings inside you. The change of the seasons - where smells, colours and nature remind you of this specific time of the year and what it means to you. Favourite places, your regular cafe or just seeing couples or families spending time together - these can trigger memories when you too shared happy times like this. Sometimes, we think of obvious times of the year that such triggers will be the strongest, birthdays, Christmas, family occasions, holiday times and the like. One of the hardest to bear is the anniversary of the death, particularly in the early years - it's common to recall all the things you did together as you count down the days to the time of the death. Sometimes you will remember every detail of the last weeks, days, hours, moments. There's no right or wrong way when it comes to grieving the loss of a loved one, as death is an inevitable part of life. There are ways to help you cope with the pain, come to terms with your grief, and eventually find a way to pick up the pieces and move on with your life. Here are a few pointers from the many I used to overcome the pain of loss; accept your loss and acknowledge your pain, understand that grief can trigger unexpected emotions. Understand that your grieving process will be unique to you. Seek out face-to-face support from people who care about you. Support yourself emotionally by taking care of yourself physically. Before losing mom, people were dying around me, but I never understood death or even felt how painful grieving someone felt. Until when death knocked on my doorstep, I experienced how sad it truly feels to lose a loved one. In most cases, people associate grief with the sadness that surrounds the death of what happened or what's befalling around them. Yet some people may or can experience distress after many other losses, including a relationship breakup, losing a job or a house to debt, having the part of the body like an arm or leg amputated. These episodes lead to a feeling of loss and can or may add an extra layer of complexity.

The Grieving Stages of Loss: Grieving is highly a one-person experience that has no right or wrong way to mourn the loss of a loved one. How you grieve depends on many factors, including your personality, coping mechanism, life experience, faith, and how significant the loss was to you or how detached you were from the person you have lost. Inevitably, the grieving process takes time. Healing happens gradually; it can't be forced or hurried, and there is no standard way or timeline for grieving. Some people start to feel better in a matter of weeks or within just a couple of months. For others, the grieving process can last for years. Whatever your grief experiences, it's essential to be patient with yourself and allow the process to unfold naturally. We all experience grief in many different ways, whereas you may experience the episodes of grief in any order and number of occasions. You may feel sad initially, move on to anger, and then return to sadness. However, the way you mourn also depends on the type of loss and the kind of support you have during the moment of grief. Take your time to grieve. Allow yourself to do it in your unique way, and no one should ever rush you when suffering. These episodes of grief don't only express what you're enduring after loss; you experience manifold episodes of grief as explained below:

The Denial Stage: Feelings of shock and denial are unavoidable in nearly every situation, even if you could foresee it happening. It's a way for your brain to begin to understand what has happened. This is when you try to convince yourself the event hasn't happened or isn't permanent. You know the facts, of course. If your spouse has died, you might accept that it happened but then believe for a time that their death means nothing to you. If your parents have divorced, you might try to get them back together even after they've moved on to other relationships. You might go back to work after a job loss thinking they didn't mean it when they fired you. The first days of lockdown were so many people were still loitering around. This was a new thing to them, and for that reason, they were still in denial until the death toll raised the bars. When the lady told me; "your mother died two months back", my mind took a while before registering it. I was in denial that she might be mistaken until I visited mom's grave and saw where she was put to rest. Even then, I still couldn't believe it was true because I refused to go to the florist to choose a wreath as that would be admitting she was dead.

The Anger Stage: You may feel angry with yourself. You might find yourself shouting at people or showing irritation at everything from minor inconveniences to significant let-downs. This type of episode can happen at any time, even after you go through a period of acceptance. The benefit of the grieving episodes is that they help you deal with the loss and move on. Anger can energise you to do just that. Some people say many words out of anger they don't mean or decide to go to the gym and hit the punching bag to release the pain. In this case, I hated everyone around mom, including my father, who separated me from her years ago because I somehow knew she wouldn't have died if we were still living together.

The Bargaining Stage: This episode brings up uncomfortable discussions that may lead you nowhere. At some point, you might find yourself trying to reclaim what you have lost. This is the part where most people often promise they will live a better life after the pain goes away. As a child, you may have promised your parents to pick up your toys and stop arguing with your little sister or brother if your divorced parents got back together. We have all bargained at some point; this could be at your workplace, with your friends and family. Reflect upon what happened around the world during the 2020 lockdown. We were given another chance to realise many things or certain behaviours such as eating out every day, going out three times a week, and when the world was in quarantine, you must've bargained to change once it's safe to presume life. Well, the bargaining chip for losing someone you love is slightly different. You might ask the Lord to give you one more last chance with your love so that you can do things differently or ask them to take you instead or the both of you to go at once, so you don't have to live in pain.

The Depression Stage: This stage can occur after a breakup with someone, after the death of a loved one, or any other type of loss. This episode might make you feel sad and cry often. You might notice changes in your appetite or sleep patterns or loss of concentration. You might have unexplained aches and pains. When it comes to grief, guilt and regret are words that get tossed around pretty regularly. We all have things we wish we'd done differently, things we wish we had or hadn't said, things we feel terrible about. When someone you love passes away, grief can strike in varying ways and vehemence. The jumble of emotions that usually accompanies the grieving process can typically lead to feelings of depression, isolation and anxiety, but also reflection and purpose because it's the realisation of the situation, combined with; I am okay, or 'I have no one left, I have other family members who will help me to cope with grieve,' I will get another job.' Reflecting upon the situation might help you to cope with these emotions.

The Acceptance Stage: You understand what you have lost and recognise how important that person was to you. You no longer feel angry about it, and you're finished with bargaining to get it back. You're ready to start rebuilding your life. Complete acceptance brings peace, but often this stage is never complete. Instead, you might feel sad during death anniversaries or angry when you feel life would work out so much better if you just had that person with you now. When you accept the loss entirely, you'll better understand the episodes of grief. Sometimes the grief process doesn't go well. The bereaved may become stuck in one stage of grief, unwilling or unable to move through the process. In a worst-case scenario, the person can continue to be angry, sad, or even in denial for the rest of their life. When this happens, some grievers tend to seek counselling before moving out of that stage. Otherwise, the intense pain might continue over many years. Also, they may miss opportunities to build a new life that can bring happiness in the here and now. Even if you don't become stuck in one particular stage of grief and loss, you might get stuck in the cycle. You move through the stages but then move back to the previous ones, never quite able to free yourself. This return to earlier stages usually means you haven't thoroughly dealt with them yet. In cases of extreme loss, this may be necessary for a time. The shock, denial, anger, and bargaining can eventually lead to acceptance.

Regret, on the other hand, is the emotion we experience when we look back on action and feel we should or could have done something differently. It differs from guilt in that we didn't know or feel at the time that we were doing something wrong, or we didn't actually have control over the situation. Also, it typically is not that we did something that falls in that morally or legally wrong category, but rather a benign action or inaction that we later wish was done differently based on an outcome. It's a situational slump that may soon pass as you move towards the acceptance stage. Grief triggers can be upsetting because they re-kindle emotions and create feelings of sadness, longing, regret, loneliness, thoughts of 'if only' and more. Often, they spring up unexpectedly to embarrass you amongst company or surprise you with their intensity. Of course, they can also bring memories of great joy and gratitude for the happiness that you had. But one of the problems for us grievers is that it's hard to know if it's okay to share these memories and feelings because those around you probably think you have moved on and you are no longer still affected by your loss. They don't know that there is nothing more comforting than being able to share and reminisce with someone, even cry with someone. Finding the right person who is sensitive to such triggers can make a real difference to the way you cope with them. Memories are where our loved ones continue to live after they are gone; it's why we hold onto anything that reminds us of them and sometimes go to places where we feel near. When a loved one dies you are forevermore at risk of their memory triggering aftershocks of the pain. But inversely, if we let them, such reminders may also fill us with warmth and comfort. For many people, the loss of a mother is more complex than the loss of a father. Not that they may have loved them any less, but the bond between the mother and child is a special one. Your mother gave birth to you. She fed you and nurtured you throughout your childhood. A mother is the one who tends to have the most responsibility for the care of the child and is at home with the children more often than the father in most cases. Your mother is the one you run to when you have had your first period. Your mother is the one you turn to when you break up with your first boyfriend or girlfriend, when you need advice or when you have a problem. Your mother is not only your greatest advocate; she is part of you. You might even look like her. She might be your best friend as well as being your mother. It is like losing a part of yourself. No one is as interested in everything you do as your mother or as proud of you as she would be.

Grief for a parent is one of the hardest things we face in life because mothers tend to hold families together. They are the ones who keep in touch with all the family members and spread the news around. They are the ones who arrange get-togethers, keep the family home together, and generally are the hub of family life. Once the mother is gone, you have to step into her role as the primary communicator and organiser. Even if you didn't have the perfect relationship with your mother, her loss can be just as devastating. You no longer have the chance to put things right, to hear her say; "I love you, son," or "I am proud of you," or everything will be ok my boy." Although the loss of a parent is a normal part of growing up, and it happens to everyone, it is no less devastating. But many people are surprised at how much it affects them. Their friends and family perhaps won't realise just how big a blow it can be, especially if they were old or ill for a long time and it was expected or unexpected sudden death like for my mother's case. Grief for the loss of a mother is one of the hardest things we face in life, but nearly all of us have to face it at some time. Everyone's grief is different, and we all have our ways of coping. We may feel some or all of the emotions of hopelessness at times, or we might just feel numb and blank. When I lost my mother, I went into a shock of denial, an episode I accommodated for far too long because I hadn't believed she was dead. I constantly convinced myself she was gone and wasn't coming back to life. I even sometimes thought she was hiding from me not to be asked any of the questions I wanted to ask her to why she didn't look for me as a child, and to why she left me to undergo through so much pain of not having her around or growing up not experiencing a mother's love. Denial can happen to anyone, even the strongest as I am. I had years of helping others cope with the episodes of grieving the loss of their loved ones, but when my mother passed, I couldn't face up to it. After several years of living with the pain of loss, my dear mother died was a relief to know she was free from suffering and at peace. However, in some strange way, my subconscious mind expected everything to be back to normal. When I moved to the United Kingdom years ago, no one knew I was grieving the loss of a mother.

On the surface, all seemed well. Life went on. I kept busy as much as I could not think of the pain I didn't know was glowing inside, and instead of letting it out, I was instead burring it deep down. Later, during my studies of Business and Human Resources Management in London, I walked into a psychology lecture where the teacher asked who loved or had a great relationship with their mother. I put my hand up and was amazed that only half the class did. Then the lecture began on bereavement. To my amazement and that of my other student friends, the happy go lucky person I usually am was in the throes of inconsolable sobbing. I was in the middle of the business strategy course with many experienced people around. I realised that I'd been in complete denial of my mother's death, had been stuck in the denial stage of grief for years and had never allowed myself to go through the grieving process. Because of my environment, there was no one ever to bring up her name in conversations or ask me how I was. Yet I was always supportive of others, but no one ever took the time to even question how I felt about losing my beloved mother. It almost felt too easy to pretend it hadn't happened. The process of bereavement certainly hadn't happened. I guess I was still in denial. It was all too easy to pretend it never happened. Once I'd let the grieving process start, it was such a relief to be able to talk about my beloved mother again and put her photo up around the house. I always felt good after talking and thinking about her again, and I knew I could do it with comfort and not for the pain of sorrow. It had all been too painful to contemplate at the time. I missed hearing her last words before she died suddenly in the hospital, and neither was I around for her burial. So, it was all too easy to get stuck in denial and not go through the normal grieving process. My advice is to get involved as much as possible with the funeral. Emails, texts and phones these days make it so much easier. It's easy with hindsight to see that I should have chosen the wreath and cried. I should've said my goodbyes in the house and cried again. There are times when it is best to allow yourself to grieve, and then you can move on. It might even be worth keeping a grief notebook to write how you feel. Perhaps if there had been around when I learnt about mom's death, I might not have shut my feelings away so much. The importance of being supported is that if you are lucky enough to have a close family member or friend in whom you can confide, you may be able to grieve without having to pay someone else half your low income, monthly wages to make you feel better. Some people, for various reasons, may need professional guidance if they get stuck in their grief or don't have any close support network. I am forever grateful I didn't have to pay any professionals to help me learn how to live my life without someone I dearly loved. The love I have for my late mother is so deep that even though I didn't grow up around her or spend as much time with her as any child would've, I still loved her endlessly and big-heartedly without conditions. I have to say the Librarian did an excellent job for being there when I needed a shoulder to lean on, and if I don't take this opportunity to thank her, I would be an A****Hole. She was there throughout the toughest moments of struggle, and she also supported me through so many episodes of grieving I wouldn't overpower without any support. However, the magnitude of which the tribulations of loss tested me was also the extent to which I was restored. I now live by the code; "it's now or never."

Before the reaper took mom away, I was less concerned with life and hadn't reached that point of realising how vital life was or how valuable everyone around me was. I was stuck in a very dark place where the fear of the unknown caused me to miss out on numerous good times I could've spent with my mother before she died because I always thought I had enough time to make enough money. My job became more important than going back to check up on my mother because I wanted to make enough money. Now I am regretting the journey not taken and all the questions I held back on the day I found my mother. It wasn't until that time that I knocked my toe against the edges of the door. Then I woke up and started appreciating everyone around me more and what I had. Over these past years, I have learned a lot from episodes of loss that each moment or minute you waste is a gone case. You can never make enough money to sustain all your needs because each time you pay your way towards a problem, new ones jump on your waggon unexpectedly. Like the death of my best friend that followed after the loss of my beloved mother, taught me the hard way that life has a way of tasting you, and it has its ways of educating you how to improve 'Oneself' and whatever wrongdoing you've done or accommodated. When you are in a state of despondency, you feel hopeless and super bummed out. When you lose a loved one or experience failure in a business, despondency can happen when you are feeling sad after the loss of a loved one. However, this doesn't only include sadness but can also occur during times when you develop a feeling of hopelessness. Thus, it's human to have an inherent desire for a sense of belonging. We all want to feel loved, accepted, and validated. I wanted to believe that my life mattered. Deep down, I wanted to belong to something bigger than myself, to feel the power. Family is, of course, the first group where we will belong. You don't get to choose which family you have, and your immediate kin's overall function or dysfunction will impact which groups you will be able to join in the future. If you come from a loving, supportive household, you will likely grow up confident and self-assured. On the other hand, if you come from an emotionally unstable family, the chances are that you will grow up fearful and uncertain. Both will affect your social status and your long-term prospects for acceptance and even prosperity.

When I thought about my family and how we grew up not sharing our feelings and emotions, I conceded I wanted to experience a positive difference. It was about the sense of belonging I hungered for, the need to be connected, the deep desire to be a part of something meaningful, something that makes a difference. I didn't even care if what I longed for to belong had positive or negative consequences in that moment of thought. Whilst grieving, in that moment of reflection. It's all about your need for belonging, which is more than what you might have thought. Understanding it can help contribute to your emotional wellbeing, and it can pave the way towards feeling better. A sense of belonging improves your motivation, health, and happiness. Connecting with others also helps you understand that everyone struggles and has difficult times. You can feel less lonely when you want to share good times with others. When you see something extraordinary, like a child's smile or a sunset, it increases your joy at the moment when you can share it with someone you care about. I was very much aware that I lacked a sense of connection as a child because the only emotional connection was with my mother. When I was separated from her, I lost that connection to share my feelings freely. I grew up around people who had their sense of connection disconnected, and none of them was emotionally available like it was with my mother. She constantly showed me how a sense of belonging could help to give a sense of meaning to someone's life. This isn't only important, but a sense of purpose can also significantly affect someone's wellbeing in numerous ways. After the separation, I spent my entire childhood feeling like my father was psychologically rejecting me. But as I grow up, I have realised that, sadly, many people experience social rejection at various times in their lives. This is often true in the case of knowledgeable people and deep thinkers like myself, given the triviality of today's society. This way of life has been part of human nature to find it difficult to accept those different from us. This can also mean that those who don't share the same beliefs and vision on life as you may reject you. You may experience rejection and exclusion at work and social or family gatherings or even see it in your children at home. This can be particularly painful if the people who misunderstand you are your family.

Being rejected or misunderstood can lead to difficulty in accepting yourself as you are. You may try to change your ways of doing things, your beliefs and behaviour just to fit into a group of people, as we used to change our cultural ways of doing things at school not to feel cut off from our true selves. A sense of belonging is essential to all human beings, including the animals we pet. Thus, if a sense of belonging can increase that, then it is something worth building and constantly working on. In the family I grew into, we were friendly to each other, but there was no bonding. The lifelong desire to feel connected and accepted by those you love. One of the fundamental needs far greater than necessities and shelter is the need to feel like you belong and you are loved by those you devote your love to. Belonging in the sense that these make you feel connected and accepted no matter the difference in cultural norms or how formidable your flaws can get sometimes. We are all human beings, but we have different levels of needs. Some greedy lads want more than what they have, and still sorrowful or haven't found that kinship and there those with less, who are contented at heart and happy with the little they possess. I have seen many people who feel lonely, yet they've got wealth they can't even count, and I believe it has to do with the fact that they don't feel like they belong. This drive for belonging never goes away and is present at all stages of our lifespan. Sometimes your motivation for belonging is lacking due to mental health problems like the depression that comes with the loss of a job, going through divorce, separation or dementia in the elderly. Or sometimes it could be the loss of a loved one that triggers your sense of connectedness like it was in my case after I lost my mother. You can work on improving your need for belonging by becoming self-aware and taking a good look at your life. It may mean we need to make some changes or talk to someone you know won't use your vulnerable state against you in future. The need for belonging evolves around our lifespan that, if you are fortunate enough to be born and raised into a family that helps or supports your goals and visions, cares about your well-being, makes you feel loved and cared for, you're truly blessed. However, if you were born in a family disconnected from devotion, you need to jumpstart your battery when at its lowest.

A teenager who feels abandoned in their younger years may not develop a sense of what compassionate love is when it comes to that time and moment of being affectionate with someone else. They may crave and search for that feeling of being accepted and cherished. This could be explored in relationships presented to them, such as in families and companions. Sometimes these relationships are excellent and helpful not just to emotionally disturbed teenagers but all of us in general because our needs can be met positively, as long as they are healthy and free from abuse. Sometimes we find comfort, acceptance and connection through unhealthy relationships. Until we are mature enough to figure out what is beneficial, we may learn the hard way. That is why it is so vital for families, no matter what the family consists of, such as a single parent, to pay close attention to their children's every need. As you mature, you learn what is healthy and not healthy for you because it benefits none other than you. As for a teenager with missed connections of love and compassion, they may end up in troubling relationships to gain the love and acceptance they're instinctually craving for. They may as well end up getting involved with the wrong crowd because they're the only ones who seem to understand and accept what it is. Look at the rate at which teenagers are joining gangs or getting pregnant at earlier stages; this could be because they never grew up with a father figure, and in that case, they feel the need to get out and search for belongingness from a male they believe can make them feel better. This brings us back to the point that our need to feel like we belong never goes away; it needs constant feeding and looked out for, just like our need for necessities, shelter, health and safety. This is because we are all human beings who constantly depend on others financially, emotionally, physically and in various ways. We do things in groups to move forward in what we do. But as we grow older and become wiser, our connections to others change due to commitments in marriage, relocating from one place to another or after finding a new phase of life. The essential personality traits remain the same, but your values and morals may change over time. Having children and starting your own family usually wakes up your moral compass. What is right and wrong suddenly becomes clear. Most people's own innate need for belonging is often met by having children. Children offer unconditional love and acceptance; the life span may change as children become more independent. Your small and sometimes growing family helps you meet your needs for feeling loved and like you belong. It also provides a sense of belonging for those who don't have children, pets, other relatives like nieces or nephews and close friends they can relate to. So how can you build that sense of connection in your life and those around you?

Building a sense of belonging might not be easy, but when implemented the right way, the results may/ might make you experience the meaningfulness of life and improve your health and well-being; it's definitely worth the effort. It's all about creating a light under a tunnel that has been dark for quite some time. On the other hand, fostering a sense of belonging isn't a one-way street, because it does go both ways. The same applies to when we attend a family gathering or meet up with friends of friends for the very first time; you may or might not feel like you belong based on your actions or the actions of the people you've just met for the very first time. For instance, when I first met the family members on my mother's side, they were having conversations I couldn't contribute to because I didn't know what exactly they were talking about. I, therefore, felt entirely left out and that I didn't belong. During my mindset and life coach sessions, I often ask clients: When something of a kind happens; do you take people as they are or avoid them? Do you feel connected or disconnected from those around you? Do you feel accepted or rejected by those you meet for the first time? Do you willingly and freely accept people you have just met, or do you tend to dislike them straightway?

We also know that loneliness and isolation are linked to depression. It's, however, not clear what came first or whether the lack of connection to others causes the two episodes. Sometimes depression can be triggered by losing a job, loved one and valuables. Those who feel a sense of belonging have good connections with others through family, friendships and other social relations. They also know whom to avoid based on how they are treated or because the person is wordy to an introvert. When considering adults, I think about workplaces and cultural or religious-based clubs. Friendships and family relationships can be and need to be, fostered and nurtured. To end isolation and loneliness brought on by feeling left out takes some effort, and it goes both ways. To improve your sense of belonging, you need to help others feel like they belong to support that connection and acceptance grows. Here are some ways to help nurture a sense of belonging:

Accept who you are: Start with loving yourself and fully accepting your flaws; you will become more confident and open to those around you. Accepting who you're helps to increase the reasonableness of finding the right people you justly belong to. You will be less likely to present a front to the world, allowing the right people to get to know the real you.

Do what you love: When you follow the things you passionately love, it helps you to connect with like-minded people in the long run. When you follow your passion and engage with the right-minded people who have the same goals, passion and energy as yours, you are 100% more likely to pursue your dreams and succeed in life. Learning to love the person you are and appreciate your accomplishments in life may lead to more meaningful relationships.

Make the right connections: Seek to connect with the right people instead of becoming more likeable to the wrong ones who will only waste your time and delay your process to grow. The moment you decide to walk with the right flock of people, you will feel connected to them because of the values and interests you share. You won't have to change your ways of doing things to fit in with the right people; you will notice that deeper relationships evolve fast because you can be yourself.

Stop seeking validation and approval: You will never receive love and acceptance from everyone no matter how hard you try. The desire to feel a sense of belonging can sometimes cause one to become a people pleaser. The same applies to being afraid to lose people; you shouldn't be scared to lose anyone. You should be afraid of losing yourself by trying to please everyone around you. Regrettably, you can't please everyone simultaneously and most definitely not all of the time. Because trying to please others only separates you from yourself, leading you to a much more painful life.

We have all found ourselves in situations where we're hated for being ourselves or realistic. I have experienced several occasions in which people hate me for who I am or for telling it as it is, but that has never bothered me because (I would rather be hated for who I am than to be loved for who I am not). We live in a society where we've to fake our feelings, identity, cultural norms, and values to fit in, and we forget to be whom we are meant to be. So, if you're among those who have been doing this, it's about time you give up trying to please everyone. Stop being a people pleaser and be true to yourself to create a healthy and meaningful life. And when you meet people for the first time, try putting yourself in their shoes and look for ways you are similar to others rather than focusing on differences. Focus mainly on what's good in people rather than seeking the bad in them. When you judge others less, you tend to feel less considered. Try to be more understanding than to be right at all times. The truth of the matter is that everyone you meet has different cultural norms, values, skills and attributes, and you can learn from them if you remain open-minded and non-judgmental. If you want to feel accepted, it helps if you're more accepting of others. This doesn't mean you have to put up with people's bullshit or their destructive behaviours, but you can act with compassion. Thus, a sense of connection is essential to humans, but sadly, we live in a society where the importance of community is undervalued. Indeed, many media sources seem keen to emphasise what makes us different and divides us rather than bringing us together. This means we are left to build a sense of community and belonging. The trauma of being separated from my mother at the age of five stuck with me for life because there's nothing, I can do to undo what was done or even change its reality. I cried myself to sleep every day that went by as I watched my relationship with my mother going downhill. Sometimes I felt lonely and wanted to be loved just like my mother would've cherished and cuddled me when in tears, but none of those around me understood being affectionate. I constantly asked myself why my father separated me from someone who loved me unconditionally, but none of the questions that crossed my mind made any sense. He was too tough, busy and distant for the both of us to have a conversation, but I guess deep down each time he looked at me.

Maybe because I was too little to understand what made them reach a point where my father couldn't even take me to see her, perhaps they didn't bother telling me precisely what was going on because my opinion as a child didn't matter, since I was a nobody. It was as if she was wiped off the face of the earth, yet she must've been worried, and there wasn't anything she could've done to change my father's mind. I remember being told about my father at a young age was that he was always travelling and very busy that he could barely come to visit me. What I knew was that before my mother's parents died. They were the most protective human beings have ever met. They were very strict that they controlled everything to a point where there was a man, they wanted my mother to marry. Some handsome fellow in the army came to our house dressed in full combat. Again, I was too little to understand what was going on. I would say, though, that she never brought guys at home for the time I lived with my mother; she respected herself and those around her. When mom's parents died, it was always the two of us, at church together, even to her workplace at the market where she had a small business, and everywhere she went. In most cases, when a child is in between a younger age difference, some parents tend to think the child is too young to acknowledge what's going around them. What most parents fail to notice is that, when a child is between the age of three and five, their brain picks up quickly from several things because they're beginning to make sense of things and for that, register everything that happens and can write a story about when they grow. This is why people grow up, and patterns from upbringing follow them around. It's like your child growing up being called all sorts of abusive words or in a household where there's too much swearing in front of the children. Don't be surprised when they disappoint you at school, during a family reunion or gathering of any kind. I grew up in a family where we never saw our parents argue about anything. I never heard my mother swear before and never heard her talking down or saying anything wrong about my father. When my father separated me from mom, he didn't notice when he took me away from her. He sabotaged my joy and took away the other part of me I will never replace to the day I perish. But before this all happened, mom was my everything. She took me everywhere she went with her, even when she had so many friends and family members where she could've left me to be babysat. I remember she always used to say; "wherever I go, you go, and whatever I eat, you eat, and if it's the poison, we then die together for as long as you're right next to me."

I still can't fathom the thought that she's no longer here with us because, before the separation, mom and I were besties who locked out for one another. She was finically struggling, but she never gave me away or sold me to a wealthy family no matter how bad the situation was. She used to say; "nothing will ever do as apart, because each time I look at you. Somehow faith is restored in me, and you encourage me to push further."

My mother was the kind of person who didn't have food in the house, and she couldn't ask for help from anyone, even when her two sisters were just a few walkable miles away from her house. I don't know how she managed to feed me, but it always happened no matter how bad life was. She never gave up on prayer, and she learned so much about God that every single evening she could go to church and practice with her singing church choir. I grew up watching how kind my mother was to other people, even those that miss treated her, that such kindness to treat people with fairness regardless of who they're or where they're from. I guess being around her most of the time and observing the things she was going through; I came to realise the strengths of women at the age of five, especially during the days I found her in a dark room by herself shading tears. And each time I walked up to her, she could quickly dry her tears and wore a big smile on her face like everything in her life was perfect. She was very good at hiding, not to show how bad things were in her life, even though I was too little to understand what was going on in her life. I could sit on her lap with a puppy look on my face to comfort her. I saw home my presence restored faith in her, and she could function again. She called me her pride and joy. I have never met someone as strong, kind, and loving as my beloved mother was. One of the biggest reasons I met the wrong women who had different intentions was because I was looking for that motherly love and ended up being used and dumped. For the fact that I lucked that motherly love when growing up, I thought I would find it in the woman I fell deeply in love with, and little did I know I was still vulnerable and fragile to go out and start seeking someone to love me. At the same time, I was approaching the most difficult episode of grieving, acceptance. I discovered that there wasn't anything I could've done to go way back and change how my life started, but I knew I had to start somewhere to change the ending. Because if I didn't, that would've eradicated me. Nonetheless, my story is filled with broken elements, the bad choices I have made, and some ugly truths. It's also filled with significant comebacks, peace in my soul and grace that saved my life. I have learned from life that for every inch of sadness lies a foot of happiness ahead. It was through sorrow and pain, I learned that the simplest of times brings the grandest of pleasures and that the hardest goodbyes often lead to the best hellos. Through the episodes of grieving, I have learned from the risky choices I made and guided me to the most unexpected discoveries, and those tough times unveiled the sincerity of people I thought were my friends but were just shadows in my paths. I have learned how to raise my head up high and hold onto a wounded smile every day that passed by until I eventually freed myself from frowning.

When your life changes, you lose the love of friends, some pieces of yourself that you never imagined would be gone. And without you realising it, these lost pieces somehow come back in numerous forms. New love enters, and better friends than the ones you had in the past come along to uplift not just your soul but everything about you. You will become stronger and happier, while the more sagacious you gawk with joy in front of the mirror. This is the new you, blessed with new beginnings in which you are allowed to change from being used to discomfort. You are now entitled to say no to what doesn't serve you. You are allowed to change your mind at any time, especially when you don't feel like it. You are very much allowed to be different from a crowd of a thousand people who want to look the same and have matching outfits or possessions. You have a choice, and for that, you can wake up from bed and decide not to do a damn thing you have done in the past. You have allowed love to flow into your bloodstream and to accept the person who has overcome all the episodes of loss. You are absolutely allowed to love whom you want to love and distance your energy far away from toxic people who aren't good or the right fit for this new life you are about to experience. You have now started letting go of unproductive people without having to explain your reasons. You have become bold and beautiful and at the same time fearless because you learned the hard way that the most dangerous thing anyone can do is to become attached to fear of any kind. You kick ass now like a martial artist who has been in a temple long enough to master the techniques of kung fu. You now laugh louder like someone who has been amused by Kevin Heart, the funniest man on earth. You no longer have any regrets whatsoever because you have accepted what it is, for what it was. You are a human being who makes mistakes because it was from your previous bad choices, you learned and took notes, and that's why you are new to you today. This is your new life, make every second count, make your own validations and paths the way you please because you're no longer that broken person you were in your past life. You are enough to become just anything because you are much stronger than you think.

The pain that didn't kill me only moulded me into a much stronger person. The more pain I bared during the grieving process and throughout all life triumphs, the little did I know I was regenerating into something larger than life itself. I became stronger every single day that passed by. I started seeing life differently when the Librarian informed me that she was pregnant. We went together for her medication at Rubaga hospital, and I was there for her throughout those nine months. Just like she was there for me while my sorrow was drowning in a pool of pain. I'm talking about pain more profound than when you drop a pretty picture frame, and it breaks, then you feel sad. The best therapy I had was the blessing of becoming a father in 2008 and onwards. I am not suggesting that you do the same or go out there and have children to feel better. I am not giving you the magic potion to self-heal or mend a broken heart. I am sharing whatever is written in this novel based on personal experiences whilst going through hell after losing my mother. Things weren't easy for me because I reached a point where I didn't believe I had a purpose in living anymore. I felt like I didn't have anything left for me even when I had a big family I grew around. At that moment, nothing mattered to me anymore. And out of the blue, the Almighty sent me an angel I nicknamed the Librarian to save me from drowning; she came at a perfect time when I honestly needed someone to show me that I still had a chance in life and there was much more to live for than thinking of ways to end my life. The thing is, the epidermic of losing a mother doesn't just go away overnight; it's a scar that stays for the rest of your adult life. Because no matter how strong you think you are, there will always be moments that drag you back to that dark corner in which you feel worthless in life. I didn't read about this. In the news or hear it from someone's story. I have lived it, and it somehow still follows me wherever I go.

The Joy of Becoming a Father: When my daughter was born on the third of March in 2008, she brought more than joy to my life. I remember standing at the bedside of the Librarian while she pushed and right after welcoming my baby girl into this chaotic world. I wanted my voice to be the first sound she listened to, something I didn't think her mom would've agreed with. But luckily enough, the Librarian somehow passed out, and that's when the doctor said to me; "congratulation, sir! It's a bouncing baby girl. Do you mind holding her for us while we patch her mother first?"

As excited as I was, I couldn't say no because, after all those nine months, I barely slept waiting for her to be delivered, or during those nine months I was called to bring fish and if I delayed more than or didn't bring what she wanted to eat within five minutes. I either had to return the food or eat it myself but from outside the house and buy something else she wanted to eat. She could call and say, 'I want to eat fish.' Then within just two minutes had passed, she could call with a changed mind, asking for something different from what she first asked. Having gone through several grief processes, I was overwhelmed to see my daughter for the first time. When the doctor handed her over to me while she was still bloody, I knew I had to be the first person to hold her in my arms. My voice was the first sound my daughter heard, and ever since that day, we built a more robust bond; not even distance can sabotage. I recited a prayer in one of her ears and said to her; "hey baby! It's me, your dad, your best friend and your protector. And I will always be your provider for as long as you need me to be."

Do you remember the first time you saw your baby? It was likely a moment of relief, amazement, and yes, a little shock, too. You had all of those same emotions, and though you might not have noticed your wife had just delivered a baby, after all, these images capture that beautiful moment when dad meets his child for the first time. Fatherhood is not rocket science, but it's also not the simplest thing in the world. Young girls who have a warm, close relationship with their dads develop into strong, confident women. When you live a life of integrity and honesty, you set a positive example for your daughter on how to handle the world. Fathers play a big role in their daughters' self-esteem, self-worth and body image. A strong father-daughter bond also plays a heavy role in her ability to express her feelings, emotions, and thoughts. As a father, you can bond with your daughter right away by taking a hands-on role in her care. As she grows, the way you interact with her will obviously change. All in all, a father-daughter relationship can have a far-reaching influence on the daughter's life. You should, therefore, make an effort to build a close relationship with your daughters. In that regard, a robust father-daughter relationship helps a girl develop healthy levels of self-esteem, security, competitiveness and femininity even competency. You benefit as much from father-daughter relationships as your daughter does. Having a daughter changes the way you behave for the better. Rest assured that there is no right or wrong way for a father to build a healthy bond with his daughter. You can choose to do it your way; the important thing is that you do it. Fatherhood won't be easy for starters, but it's a perfect father-daughter bonding timeline that involves; the first challenging twenty-four months of a diaper change, feeding, bathing, dressing, and reading to her. Don't insist she plays with pink called girl's toys. From toddler to preteen years. You will pretty much play silly games of cooking and tea parties and play with barbies. This can be annoying at times, but it's all worth the experience in the end. Be there for her like a dad is supposed to be. All you have to do is to introduce her to sports, even male-dominated ones.

Get involved in her school activities, field trips, sports teams and projects. Work together around the house and teach her how to make and fix things. Don't make gender comparisons that imply that femininity is somehow inferior. When your daughter reaches her teen years. Be a role model she expects you to because your contribution makes a great impact I her upbringing. The qualities you embody will influence your daughter's future relationships with men. When things become overwhelming, discuss and come to an agreement with your partner about tough topics like sex, the extreme dress that might put her at risk, the use of drugs and risk-taking, then be prepared to talk with your daughter when these issues come up. Your ultimate goal as a father is to help her learn to make good decisions and say no to things that don't add up and not just because daddy said so. Don't focus only on her looks; pay attention to what your daughter says, thinks, feels and dreams to become. Understand that her appearance is one aspect of her whole person, so don't be afraid to tell her she looks pretty. Don't encourage dieting. Instead, promote healthy eating and exercise because it boosts morale, self-esteem and mental health without the fear of fitting into society's body standards. Setting a good example for your daughter goes beyond teaching good manners and time management skills. Here's how to be a role model who raises a resilient woman. Children learn good behaviours by copying good examples, and moms play a huge role in those everyday moments when our children pick up on what we moms do or say. The problem is you never know what they are tuning in to. That's why it's important to monitor your own behaviour and intentionally start to model the type of behaviours you hope your daughter will copy. Becoming a new parent causes you to change as an individual. You become someone new in a way that makes you do things for the good of your child or children because, as mentioned above, children like coping with what their parents do or say.

Change is often a complex process that is unavoidable when you become a new parent. We often succumb to shiny object syndrome because almost everything has become a distraction. However, nothing can be accomplished if there aren't any hoops jumped. It's essential to identify the end goal, create a plan to make it happen, and then remain focused on that plan moving forward. When it's time for a change, there isn't anything you or anyone can do to stop it from happening. A lot happens during this time of change. When I relocated to go and live in London, I knew I was leaving a piece of my heart behind. It was hard not taking my children with me to London. Whenever I visited them, I wished the time could move slowly to spend as much time with them as possible. But that's one thing man can't control, and that's to stop time from going further. I have to say; it takes a while and a lot for a man to cry, but watching my children staying behind and apart away from me for the first time. Real tears were revealed and have continuously poured during that goodbye at the airport. It always starts with a teardrop, then the other, followed by the other, and before you know it, the entire team is shading a tear or two. My children always told me not to leave them behind, and they had every right to say so, but little did they know there was a sure thing I had to follow for such a thing to happen. Sometimes I wished all destinations were visa-free, and then the reality of it kicked in, and I snapped out of such childish thoughts. Raising my children from miles away has been the second most challenging task in my life. Apart from my children for eleven years is the second great experience a loving parent can ever go through. As a father, I want my children to grow beside me and have everything I never had. I want them to try out so many things I never tried, but because they live miles away from me, it's seemingly impossible for it to happen. Whenever I see another man showing love to their children, I envy that and get a mixture of loneliness and mixed emotions; then tears start pouring down on me, which always leads to calling out my late mother's name. I always look at my late mother's picture I have hung on the wall and say; "but why mother, why."

We sometimes forget the depth of connection we have with our parents. They are often our main connection in the world and to the world. Even if we have a loving spouse, children and many close friends, the death of a parent means the loss of one of our first and most important connections. The misconception that a mature and capable adult will not need to grieve their parent can cause the bereaved to feel even more alone, as their grief goes unrecognized. After our parents die, we take another look at them. We realize, perhaps for the first time, all they did for us as children. For some of us, when we become parents, we appreciate the challenges our own parents must have gone through. We gain a new perspective on their lives. If we idealized our parents when we were kids, now we also see their flaws and imperfections. In the case of losing one parent, for instance, your mother, there is a great opportunity to get to know more about her from the perspective and experiences of your surviving father. In our adulthood, our relationship with our parents changes and continues. Before a parent is gone, we understand intellectually that they will die someday. But understanding and anticipating does not prepare us for the grief we feel when as an adult we lose a parent. As you reflect on the memory of your loved one, whether you are alone or walking through it with a surviving parent as mentioned above, you are beginning the journey through the now well-known stages of grief. At the beginning of 2020, I was at home relaxing on my day off. I scrolled through my social media platforms to find better ways to best promote my novels. God knows why. I came across this video of one of Simon's got talent shows. An eleven-year-old boy who played the violin of the song 'what doesn't kill you makes you stronger. Before he leant to play, he mentioned being bullied at school by students because he had cancer. His family was worried he might die of cancer. But the energy he had on stage when being questioned was inspiring when he started playing. The crowd went bonkers while tears walked a mile my cheeks and the aisle of my nose down to my lips like a river that never runs dry. As a loving parent, thoughts run down to my babies, and I started blaming myself for how helpless I was to help them with anything they needed. I cried in silence, not to be heard by the Romanian guy talking on the phone not far from where I was. When you're at the edge of losing hope, the universe has its way of sending you signs, not to give but slow down on overthinking. To reflect on everything, you've and those who are there for you. You are always finding something useful to do and somewhere to go on a trip, but the most significant gifts are already in your possessions. Give presence in these moments, especially who you are. Pay close attention to your thoughts and heart because those to remain silent listen more than those who interrupt. Listen to what your mind and body need and your golden heart. Reflect only on what matters most, and forget about the things that add nothing but pain and misery to your life. Be bold enough and brave because deep reflection is the most arduous journey ever taken, but to those who persist, it's the most rewarding at the end of a dark tunnel.

The Memorial Service: Growth comes with great wisdom and responsibilities, and responsibilities come with a great experience. Growth isn't about living from some destination far from those you love or far from home. It's about the little day to day changes that pump your blood to the last vein and make you feel a little more joy, like the ones that make you feel a little lighter at heart and more like you. I have learned that growth knows no destination because it's more of a direction towards becoming more aligned with your authentic self. It's about directing you towards whom you want to become. If you face any changes in your direction, that's perfectly okay, too, because growth doesn't happen in a straight line. There are always zigzag lanes, potholes, and a couple of hoops to jump before anything makes sense or before the picture becomes much clearer ahead. Growth ebbs and flows push you into a formidable person. Growth is about doing what you think is the best today to make tomorrow more joyful and the tunnel ahead brighter. One early morning I received a call from my mom's sister asking me to go to the village with her. She didn't say precisely what it was we were going there for, but she asked me to come along with enough cash to help out on a few things. As someone who was still looking for answers, I agreed without hesitation. The following day I woke up early before the birds started chirping and took a taxi to the agreed meeting point. I am good at timekeeping whenever it comes to meeting up with someone. I, therefore, got there an hour before the agreed time but she hadn't arrived yet. I sat down in a nearby cafe and ordered breakfast and a cuppa while waiting for her to arrive. Like most women, she wasn't good at timekeeping. She must have spent a lot of time trying on different dresses. But that didn't bother me much because I grew up around many sisters who used to take their time wearing makeup. We could sit and wait for hours while they worked on their passports. As one of my late grandmas used to say, a woman's passport is her face, and the better she looks, the more doors she opens. This reminds me of when my second mom asked us all; "who wants to go shopping with me?"

Oh boy, oh boy! We harshly fought each other for that spot like angry cubs, and then if you were chosen. Afterwards, you would regret having accepted to come by because once we got the markets. My second mom, who raised me into the man I'm today, could enter every shop to shop, and she went into detail with everything she came across that you wished you teleported back home instead. On the other hand, we all loved her treats after shopping; she was the best at giving treats and recognising a child's efforts. Because as soon as we sat down for a snack or two, you could eat anything you wanted to pay up for the time you waited while she entered from one shop to other like someone who was on a therapeutic session. Those were a few of the memorable days to remember about my childhood, which I somehow believe might've caused me to procrastinate looking for my biological mother. People walked into the cafe, and each time I saw someone from afar, I thought she would be the next one to walk right in. I reached a point where I became fed up with waiting for my late mom's sister, who wasn't showing up like she was supposed to. I couldn't take it anymore, and I was in the middle of thinking about what to do; that's when the thought of bailing up on her double-crossed my mind. I got up, and as I was about to walk out of the cafe, she eventually showed up, saying to me; "if I were in your shoes, I would probably do the same, to get up and walk out of that door."

"You are damn right you would. Riddles aside, what took you so long anyway." I added.

"You know how it is, I got stuck in traffic," she replied.

"You should've travelled earlier as I did." I angrily said.

"Don't bite my head off, right. I forgot to charge my phone and the power went off before I could even think of it." She replied.

"Why are we going to the village this urgently, did another family member I know of die?" I asked.

"Nothing like that. The rest of the family organised a memorial service to commemorate the life of seven family members including your mother. And I thought not to leave you behind this time." Mom's sister replied.

"So, what stopped you from telling me about this in advance?" I asked.

"Well! Your mother wasn't someone who disbelieved in memorial services because the religion she practised didn't allow them to disturb the person once they're dead or in their afterlife. They should be forgotten and not even go to their grave to mourn their death." Mom's sister added.

"I have never heard of such a thing before," I added.

"It's because you've been apart from us for so long." She responded.

"Well! Your mother lived that life, and up to this day, her

husband has never visited your mom's grave since she passed, and he didn't even show up on the day of her burial and memorial service. It's like she never existed to him." She added.

"That bastard!" I angry said.

"It's strictly his religion, but he is a good and kind man." She replied.

Shortly, we started the journey as we were supposed to in the first place. While on our way we talked about the religion my mom was practising, and it seemed more complicated than I thought. But who was I to judge when my life wasn't that perfect either? However, much I was in denial, I forcefully had to accept what it was and see its reality for what it was. Mind you, I hadn't finished working on my mom's graves yet because I kept on procrastinating. A weakness I carried with me for a long time was losing me spending good quality time with my late mother. On the other hand, I've to say that her death was a straight-on wake-up call. Consequently, I was there and then cut down on procrastination. We reached the village where the memorial service was going to take place three hours later. The whole place was fully packed with cars and people I didn't know. On approaching, I immediately felt small because I only knew three people by name and face. My mom's sister showed me where to sit, the one I cane with and her brother we visited when I came to the village to confirm my mother's death. I sat down and waited patiently for the ceremony to begin. The Mc did a lot of talking, and on reading out the names of those the memorial service was intended for, my mom's name wasn't read. At first, I thought the MC might've forgotten to include mom's name on the list. When I looked over the MC's shoulders, I saw how the ceremony was planned, and mom wasn't on the list, I figured this might've been because of the religion she practised. Then in my head, I was like, maybe the organiser and the rest of the clan felt like there was no need to add mom to the list because her husband and other children weren't around, and they didn't believe in memorial services due to religion. I quickly asked around until I was directed to where the ceremony's organiser was. When I approached him, he knew whom I was before opening my mouth and that's when he said; "oh my God! I last saw you when you were about this small."

"I was too young then, to remember you," I responded.

"You carry your mom's resemblance around like a woman's purse. I am hoping you give birth to a child who will carry that image well, like yourself." He added.

I stood there speechless because I didn't know what to say to someone who seemed to know me so satisfactorily. But on the other hand, I didn't want to miss out on another opportunity. I pulled him aside and asked him; "how can I contribute for my mom to be added to the group memorial service list?"

"I am glad you asked. We're short on kitchen supplies, which I don't think will be enough for such a big number of people." The organiser replied.

"For as long as you add mom to the list, just count that done," I responded.

"Please don't get me wrong, but we didn't add your mom to the list because she wasn't a true believer of such occasions. Of which no one in her family came to celebrate with us. And to be fully honest with you, if you didn't approach me, I wouldn't have added her on the list." The organiser said.

"Why are you telling me all this?" I curiously asked.

"I am telling you not to think of everyone on your mother's side as ruthless people." The organiser added.

He flipped the pages on the clipboard he was holding, among other things. Without hesitation or asking any of the family members for permission, he added mom's names onto the service list. And as soon as he finished, he showed me the page to prove it was a done deal. When I reached my hand inside one of my pockets to count how much I would give them for the supplies they needed in the kitchen. The organiser gave me a thirsty look, the one that seemed like the money wasn't going to reach whoever was in charge of the kitchen. He slightly scratched his head, and he said exactly what proved how right my thoughts were; "you can give me the money, and I will pass it on to the person in charge of the kitchen."

"Do you even know what exactly is missing in the kitchen?" I curiously asked the organiser of the ceremony.

"You've made a valid point. Ok, come with me and I will point you in the right direction." The organiser replied.

"That sounds like a solid plan, let's go." I added.

He walked with me to the back of the house, and he directed me with a point of a finger to the person who was in charge of the kitchen while saying; "go and give the money to the person in the red dress, you don't need to say anything else she will know what the money is for and she knows who you are."

The organiser went back to running the show as he was supposed to, and I walked, heading towards the direction in which the person he directed me was standing. Before I even approached the lady, she started screaming with excitement; "banange kabuladda. Ngansanyuse okukulaba."

A hug would have made a perfect impression or physically shown how excited she was to see me. Still, the reality was that hugs to most Ugandans weren't effective back then, but you could tell by the look on someone's face that they were indeed excited to see you, and this lady who was in charge of the kitchen was excited to see me. She gently held my hand, and we walked together until we reached a corner with a perfect shade where we sat down on the bench while she praised how I resembled my mother. We talked about many things, and most of them related to her childhood with my mother. She was so easy to talk to, and she made me feel like I ultimately fit into their family. She went ahead and told me that she was mom's heir. Then as we were still there talking, I asked her; "how did you get to know mom so well, yet I have never heard of you before?"

I was born alone to a mother who worked in Kenya at Kenyatta hospital as a nurse, and it might've been hard for them to mount. The two lovebirds remained in a long-distance relationship for a long time that we barely saw her, and for that and many other reasons, my parents became separated. A few months later, she was promoted to senior nurse, and because of the extra responsibilities, she couldn't make the travels from Kenya to Uganda. She called one of her friends who came and took me to live with my grandma, who loved me unconditionally like her own child. So, I grew up most of my life with my grandma. Things were so good that grandma made me feel loved and cared for like my absent mother would've done. Until when things started becoming ugly for me, but like any other family out there, things aren't always straightforward or moving on a straight line. Some crooked lines and shallow portals can swallow a living soul within a blink of an eye. When other grandma's daughters realised, I was living there and that my absent mother was regularly sending upkeep money. They all dropped off their children one by one until the number got to teenagers who lived under the care of grandma. The love she had towards me and the money mom sent for my upkeep had to be shared among other cousins. I went from someone who did nothing to someone who did almost everything at home. That each time anyone wanted something to be done, it was me they called out loud. I had no one to report to what was happening to me, and grandma was too lovely to believe my cousins were evil little brats. At first, I thought of it as pain in a broad sense but little did, I know she was grooming me into the person I'm today. When school started, things started becoming worse, that I couldn't live for school until when house chores were done and whenever my mother bought me plenty of clothes, items and a mathematical set to use at school. Everything was taken away from me and given to their children, and if I browsed or used what my mom bought me. My cousins harshly punished me for touching what they called 'their staff.' But the reality of it was that the things I was punished for or accused of stealing were personally bought for me by my absent mother. By then, we didn't have phones to call my absent mother and inform her about what was going on in the village, and I couldn't write a letter because there was no way the person would deliver it without having to first read through it. I, therefore, became stuck in my own problems. So many sinful things happened to me, where I couldn't eat food until everyone's clothes were washed and the house was spotless. Sometimes I had to collect water from a five miles radius and had to do the dishes before eating my food while my cousins ate on time, the food that my absent mother bought. Back then, parents didn't know how to care about a child's mental well-being emotionally. Whenever a child acted in a way that asked for help, they thought of it as seeking attention. One day I was sent to fetch water, five miles from where we lived. Unluckily enough, I came back after six hours had passed; this was because the water in some wells around the village had dried up that everyone had to go to one location where I fetched water and a few nearby residents. When I returned home, I was punished to never forget this moment to the day I die. Grandma didn't even ask why I was late; she just punished me and denied me food for the entire day. The sad part about this was that I was forced to watch while they ate their food, and after I washed the dishes on an empty stomach, I was grounded in my room until further notice, and this is how your mother came into the picture. She came to the room with a full plate of food, and she said to me; "not all of us are heartless. I wouldn't say I like how you are being treated as if you don't belong. But there's little I can do to help you. However, I have managed to sneak some food for you, and I am praying no one catches me offering my help."

"You are a life-saver," I added and ate the food so fast as if I was on a mission impossible scheme. I finished the food within just a few minutes because I was starving.

"For the love of God, please don't tell anyone about this ever." She added.

She continued doing the same thing for me every time I was in trouble, and ever since then, we developed a close friendship. She always covered for me, and I did the same for her. She even started helping me with house chores whenever grandma went to the garden. Then two weeks of her helping me out with chores, other cousins became jealous of our growing bond and the friendship we had, and they reported us for cooperating. I remember it was noon that day; grandma punished me and sent me to fetch water at a distance of five miles and fill up four twenty-litre petroleum tanks before four-post merīdiem. She spat saliva onto the ground, and she told me if you come back when the sun has caught up with that spot where the saliva is, count yourself dead. That was the most arduous task given to me by the grace of God. I somehow pulled this off well, and I managed to fill up all empty petroleum tanks we used to store water in before evening time. Growing up without your biological mother has many challenges that come with it, and the situations entangled can be disturbing for a child. The experience alone consumes your entire childhood and makes you feel as if you're always left out. When a child experiences traumatising moments, they often undergo a series of panic reactions which may include; flight, freezing, crying, hands in fists, desire to punch, rip, tight jaw, grinding their teeth, snarl, fight in eyes, glaring, fight in voice, willingness to stomp, kick, smash with legs, feet, feelings of anger or rage, brutal suicidal thoughts that can sometimes lead to cutting themselves to feel the pain, knotted stomach or nausea, burning stomach or metaphors like bombs and volcanoes erupting. We tend to forget that anger is indicated to make the person receiving the information being communicated feel uncomfortable. Some people might use anger to get you to pay close attention, and it's meant to feed you information. When presented with anger by our children, we should consider how we can help our children and ourselves regulate and express anger healthily. So, rather than yelling at your child for expressing signs of rage, it's better to sit them down and ask them what is wrong or what they want that very moment. When a child portrays signs of anger, it helps them get their needs met. It's how they communicate to their parents when something is wrong or missing, especially whenever they feel unheard, unseen or unimportant. This anger might provide the space to say to someone I feel unsupported by you, can you help me. You might be surprised to know that anger helps you discover boundaries, such as that feeling that grows when your boss brings you another quick job. The boundary may be. 'I am overwhelmed', and a response could be 'I cannot take on extra work.'

Your teenager may feel it when you ask them about a relationship or inquire about their day as a parent. Their perimeter maybe 'I want some space or privacy,' and a response could be, 'I don't want to talk, right now. I need some quiet time.'

The thing is, anger has informed us, and we have set the boundary. It has somehow even helped us to get things accomplished. Some of us might be motivated by being told, "you can't do that.'

Your response might be, 'watch me! Or right, I will show you,' and off we go to prove a point. Would we have achieved any of this without that sense of anger?

Presumably Not! When a child's trauma response is to fight, they are in the midst of trauma on top of trauma. They will likely be easily provoked and rapidly escalate emotionally, resulting in massive tantrums, destructive behaviour, or prolonged yelling or screaming. What some parents don't pay attention to is that; when it comes to any kind of teaching. Suppose a child has only lived in chaotic environments, where they frequently witnessed domestic violence or other types of conflict between caregivers. In that case, they will likely lack tools for healthy emotional regulation. If they have seen a lot of yelling and raging, they are more likely to yell and rage. Nobody likes to feel angry, but we all experience the emotion from time to time. Given that many adults find it hard to express anger in healthy and productive ways, it's unsurprising that angry feelings often bubble into outbursts for children. Most parents find themselves wondering what to do about tantrums and angry behaviour, and more than a few wonder whether the way their child behaves is normal. However, everyone experiences anger in response to frustrating or abusive situations, most anger is generally short-lived. No one is born with a chronic anger problem. Rather, chronic anger and aggressive response styles are learned. There are multiple ways that people learn an aggressive, angry expression style. What you might take from this is that anger is often the result of another feeling being activated. This might be hurt, fear, embarrassment, disappointment or, rejection; the list is endless. When you feel angry, your body responds with intense feelings. These are often physical. You will probably see the body move into a fight, flight or freeze mode, which is the physiological reflex process that enables you to survive from danger. This reflex involuntarily triggers various hormones to flood into your systems, increasing your heart rate, tensing your muscles and giving you a surge of energy from the adrenaline and cortisol that gets released.

We are, in fact, wired for action. What we find in children and teenagers when they go through this surge of hormones is that they often don't know what to do next and what happens is usually not a conscious decision. This is not to excuse the behaviour but to explain it. When I lost my mother to cancer at the age of eight, my life was shattered into misery and pain. And ever since then, I became angry with everyone because nothing made sense anymore. Even though she was absent, I was happy knowing she was alive, and one day I could go and visit her and tell her all my secrets. But the thought of knowing she wasn't going to come back and I wasn't going to say to her what was happening in my life broke my heart. I became aggressive; I started missing school and self-harming as I struggled to deal with episodes of grief. I could sit in the corner with a laser blade and cut my arm until it bleeds pretty bad. I lost interest in everything I loved doing to make my mother feel proud of me. I didn't care about anything anymore. I wouldn't say I liked the village we lived in because the only person who cared about me had died, and the people I lived with didn't know how to nurture my broken young heart. Because for them, whatever I did wrong, they thought of it as seeking attention. I went from someone who loved school to someone who hated even looking at the uniform. I utterly became traumatised by my mother's death that I even started talking back whenever my grandma asked me to do something. I became stubborn to the point where I was punished for my actions every day. Some adults don't think of you as someone who needs professional help when you're a child because they don't think children also grief. Things got worse, and my grandma had to summon my father. When he came to the village, grandma explained to him what was going on, and he decided to take me with him to Kampala city for a couple of days. When I got there, things were different. My father always spoke of my mother, and he always showed me her pictures to set my mood right. He might not have been a psychologist, but he knew what to say to put me in line. Good days run pretty fast, and before I knew it was time for me to go back to the village. When he informed me the day he would take me back to my worst nightmare, I cried my eyes out and begged him not to. My mother's dying wish was for me to grow up in the hands of my grandma. She believed grandma was capable enough to teach me traditional morals to help me grow into a respectful woman, which men won't take lightly. She technically had full custody of me; thus, he couldn't just say yes to me to upset my grandma. He, therefore, promised me, "let's go back to the village and if your grandma gives me the green light. There won't be any reason why you won't come and live with me in the city."

I might have been young then, but that seemed like a good deal, which I very much agreed to. We, therefore, went back to the village the next day, and he officially asked my grandma whether I could go and stay with him in the city, something she agreed to without hesitation. My life got to a whole new level when I reached Kampala, city. I was sent off to a nearby private boarding school, where I made loads of friends who cheered me up and just like that, my life transformed, knowing I still had a father who cared and loved me unconditionally. What most grownups don't understand is that as a child, when you lose a loving parent, all you need is for someone to be there emotionally and not to be treated lightly like someone who doesn't have feelings or as if being a child means you can't have emotional distress. The moral of the story is that sometimes young children need to be supported without adults being judgemental and fussy about their children's emotional needs. She told us about her life story and how she developed a friendship with my late mother. Later on, I walked back to the tent to attend the ceremony where I got to meet mom's heir, someone I spoke with very briefly because there were so many people waiting to talk to her, so I didn't waste too much of her time. Even though I didn't get enough time to ask my mom's heir questions, the memorial service went well. When the memorial service ended, there were only a few people left. I looked around for mom's sister to say goodbye, and I couldn't find her. So, I left the village and returned to being the tearful broken person again. Days followed, and I started dreaming about my mother drowning in a pool of water, but each time I reached my hand to save her, she disappeared into a pitch-black room. The dream was scary and too complicated that I honestly failed to understand the meaning of the same tenacious dream. I became disturbed by it, to the point of being afraid of sleeping. Therefore, I came up with an idea to change my scenery. I organised a trip to Stockholm, Sweden, where I found a Polish Swedish gorgeous woman in the pub, she was so lovely but by the time I met her I had already spent beyond my budget and was staying in a hostel. She desperately wanted to fuck my brains out, but for some reason, she couldn't take me to her house, and I didn't ask why either. She came to the hostel a day before returning to London, and there was this couple inside and a ninety pounds woman with smelly feet and a loud snore that kept almost everyone awake. We kissed, and I felt her like she asked me, but on the other hand, I was pocketless even to afford a pack of condoms, and just like that, I turned down being laid whilst on holiday. She seemed thirsty and in need of being dicked so bad. She hugged me, and she said: "I like that you don't take your life for granted."

"Protection comes first," I responded, and she grunted with anguish.

"It looks like fate wasn't on our side, but soon I will organise a holiday to come and visit you in London, but I will be coming with my gay friend." The Polish woman in her 20's added.

"We shall see." I said to her.

When a few days passed after I had left Stockholm, she asked for my address within areas of Baker Street, opposite Madame Tussauds, London. A request I indirectly declined because I didn't want to give out my address to a stranger, I only met for one night in a foreign country. Of which, in my head, I was afraid to end up like people who vanish mysteriously. Plus, I didn't want to end up like a friend of mine back in our teenage years, who once brought home a takeaway, and she robbed him squeaky clean that she left him sleeping naked on a metallic bed. She immediately blocked me from all channels of communication right after refusing to share my address, and that's how I learnt that; some people will only like you if you fit inside their box. Don't be afraid to shove that box up their ass. Right after the Polish, Swedish girl child ghosted me. I continued to hunt for a connection because I desperately needed someone to make me feel holly again. But little did I know the further I desperately longed for love, the more weirdos I came across. Back then, when it came to finding love, luck was the list of things on my side. I guess it was because I was an amateur who didn't know how to put in words and timid, a combination that doesn't tend to stand well in the same circle. Followed by Copenhagen, Denmark, around 2016, where I voyaged to catch up with an old friend who didn't show up or even call me back to say he wasn't able to, and he has never explained why he ghosted me. Both experiences helped me see the picture from a different perspective and knocked some senses into me. When I returned to London, the dream came to me again, and this time I could see mom's face floating on the water's surface. I gave the dream all my thought, and days after, I came to understand what it meant. I immediately organised a trip to Kampala, Uganda, to finish mom's internal house. I'm telling you! When her grave was finally refinished, I stopped having dreams of her drowning, and I felt an offload of a heavy burden off my shoulders. At the start of 2017, I stumbled upon a beautiful Norwegian woman in her 20s via a famous online dating site. We communicated daily, even though we hadn't met because of how far we were from each other. Considering how desperate I was, I organised a trip to Oslo, Norway, to go there for a weeks' holiday, but unfortunately, the girl child didn't show up. I didn't take it to heart; instead, I used that as an experience anyone can go through, and I seized the opportunity to enjoy the sceneries of Oslo, Norway. When I returned to London a week later, I had already moved on with my boring life. I was at university then, and all I cared about was getting good grades and making enough money to ensure my needs and those I care about. Friends in class thought I was gay, not that being one is a crime. But because I always came back home from work and university. I had no real life as the one I lived in seemed dull to those who saw me each time I stepped out of my house. One day I was introduced to a vibrant girl in her late 20's at a friend's birthday party next door. She was an Italian lesbian who was still keeping her identity a secret. She was originally from Sicily, where she lived with her mother and grandfather. She told me all about it after we were both high than a kite. She had never gone black before, and she was desperate to try a black mamba and see what it was all about; we, therefore, decided to head back to my place. Everything seemed normal. Sex was good, and then we got to talking. Since we were both high, we started talking about death and what happens to your body after you die, and she asked me whether I had ever thought about killing anyone. I could sense a creepy story coming my way and just shook my head. She eerily self-narrates how she has always thought about killing someone by suffocating them with a pillow or how it would feel to stick a sharp knife into their proximal artery. At that point, my heart was puckering my asshole since we were on the bed and there were two pillows around us. Of course, I was majorly creeped out, and the feeling grew as she kept on staring at me with evil gothic eyes. All in all, it was a profoundly disturbing experience. I regrated having broken the rule of not having one-night stands in my house, but that couldn't reverse the fact that it happened, and I could be punished for my sins. I became convinced I wouldn't see the sunrise the following day from that point on. I turned around and pretended to be asleep, but with one eye slightly open.

Shortly after, when a couple of hours passed, she left without a goodbye. Not that I cared; she didn't leave me a note, I was just relieved to feel my heart still beating in my chest, and I was still breathing. I stayed in the house for a couple of days, scared not to stumble into her at the coffee shop or in passing, until when I felt it was ok to go out again. As someone with high self-confidence, I feel quite comfortable interacting with other people, especially whenever I travel to a foreign country I have never been to. Indeed, I find the company of strangers very stimulating because I enjoy meeting new people. My relaxed demeanour in groups makes people around me feel comfortable. I feel confident talking to people who enjoy being around me and perceive me as socially competent. The confidence that helps me to feel comfortable talking to people also spills into my own personal beliefs about myself. Although I have several strengths because I also acknowledge and accept my weaknesses. But unlike some people, I take full responsibility for my actions. I rarely regret things I've done in the past and am not embarrassed easily. Perhaps the defining feature that sets you apart from most people is the exceptionally high standards you set for yourself. Your competence in social gatherings and at work should provide ample evidence for this. With these characteristics, it's very likely that people come to you for advice and generally think of you as someone with leader-like qualities. When you have been double-crossed so many times, you get to a point where you think of either quitting the search for someone to love you or keep going and then at the end of that thought; you come to realise that both do hurt. And that's why sometimes you need to look at things from a different perspective.

This is because you might never know why the person has decided to say no, and there are always many unforeseen reasons why people are the way they're or why they behave a certain way.

The greatest lesson I have learned in life is never to rush falling into an agreement when your conscious mind says otherwise or become involved in a relationship with someone out of desperation because people become hurt broken. When the Italian one-night stand left, I took a break from looking for love out of desperation, and I focused all my energy on bettering myself. But as we all know, their life demands you can't just ignore, especially the loneliness which doesn't know boundaries however much you express your valid reasons. Once in a while, I visited dating sites to see if I could be matched with a potential someone special to my heart. And still, my luck was limited. A year later, I came across this Kuwaitan humble Muslim girl online. We communicated almost every minute of the hour and face timed whenever I got a chance. I am the type of person who likes to keep my relationships personal to avoid other people from pocking their big noses into my business or private life. She always wanted me to face time her to show her how beautiful London was or the areas in which I was. She had never been to London, and she always spoke about wanting to come, but for some reason, her strict father couldn't allow her to travel by herself unless the entire family members accompanied her. She lived a life like a princess because her father was fully loaded. However, that wasn't why I chose to share my life story with her. She was this innocent, sweet person who came from a solid believing family of the Islamic faith. Her father was so uncompromising to the point that he wanted to be the one to choose her, the man she would spend the rest of her life with. Something her mother disagreed with, but she was powerless to challenge what it was. I asked to go and visit her because we hadn't met in person, but she refused me too because she was scared of how strict her father was and frightened of what he would've done if he had met us hanging out together. She loved talking to me because I let her be herself without being judgemental or critical until things went south for the both of us. I was on facetime with her, and little did she know her father was standing somewhere in the corner listening to every bit of our conversation. He grabbed the phone off her out of hunger and told me; "I want you to stay the hell away from my daughter."

I never spoke to her again; moving forward, I just continued living my life and went to Madrid, the capital of Spain, and many other trips that followed before doing any final touches on my mother's internal home. But of all holidays I've been up to, the recent trip to Prague during the pandemic was the most fascinating among all. Prague, a famous capital city of the Czech Republic, was previously known as the Heart of Europe for its well-preserved architecture. Whilst on holiday, I learnt that; the city bloomed in the 14th century under the Luxembourg dynasty during the reign of Charles IV, when Prague became one of Europe's largest and wealthiest cities around the 1320s. Putting the country's history aside, while the rest of the world was at the start of implementing tactical plans to stay safe during the epidermic of COVID-19. On the 12th of March 2020, the Czech Republic was already a ghost town, everything from restaurants to shopping malls were all closed, and locals were at home in their homes. A few countable corner shops were open, and the likes of countable fast-food chains created emergency takeaway windows for precaution. Oh! What a holiday? But as a storyteller who is very much intrigued by heart-pumping Architecture and cultural differences, I was very much looking forward to visiting Prague because of its historical architecture built in the Golden Ages. I met a few locals in my hostel, but I couldn't tell whether they were racial or they were practising social distancing. We all have issues because we all have a story. And no matter how much work you've done on yourself, we all snap back sometimes. So be easy on yourself. The scars you can't see are the hardest to heal. Growth is a dance, not a light switch. So, no matter how wretchedly unhappy you are, the stormy weather you are going through, the unprecedented circumstances you have or still facing in life. There will always be something good coming your way. Remember that! Don't ever let life beat you to appoint where you lose hope. Believe me not; there's light at the end of the tunnel, waiting for you to shine bright like a diamond. Speaking from experience, I have been rejected by women with or without children multiple times just because I have four beautiful children. I felt as if my life was lacking, like someone with saggy gynecomastia groaned under my weight or someone who won't be loveable again. Honest to God/ Allah, I almost gave up on many occasions, but a silent voice deep down argued me to keep pushing and never give up on myself. I stood by my belief that one day somebody's daughter would come and shower me with unconditional love. I have always unluckily met women who wanted to use me as their spam donor or as a sex baby-making machine. Witnessing that in the past, I learnt from experience and took notes clear enough to electrify my senses.

Years later, after having gone through a line-up of dating apps and having met women with sex desires and unknown intentions. I am delighted to say; I have finally found someone to share laughter with. She's the only special someone to have lifted my Melancholy of years that followed the loss of my beloved mother. She makes me feel like I am sleeping in a blue sky on holiday, far away from searching and scheduling meetings with cock thirsty whores. Looking at her beautiful smile, she makes a bad day turn into a bright one. She came into my life when I less expected it to happen, but at the same time as when I needed devotion most and at a great timing when desperation was at its lowest. The beauty of it all is that; there's a good thing going on between us, but it's always fascinating to see an outsider showing interest when you're in a fulfilling relationship with someone. That makes you wonder where these admirers were hiding when single. When you are single, people disbelieve in you because they don't think you have got the guts to fulfil their desires until you slam the actual truth right into their faces. The weirdest thing about the devil is that this bastard doesn't sleep because he hates to see smiley faces. He loves shitting on heads and ruining good things or perhaps continues keeping the weak hearted in the temptation of misery. So, don't let that fool you, especially after finding someone special. And if she can suck you dry, play with your balls and cook you a meal after a long day. My friend, hold on tight to that special someone because real is rare nowadays. People come into your life with some inexplicable intentions, and don't let those momenta distractions miss guide you from the right cause. When you are young and energetic, you become dependably comfortable with your life or current position, and you tend to take things for granted. Thus, you waste a lot of time procrastinating. Before you know it, you are in your 30s with lots of responsibilities, miss connections and possibilities. You regret the time you wasted all along and the opportunities you missed or refused to take because you were still young, wild, and accessible. My exact point is if you get a chance to develop, don't wait for church bells to ring because time waits for no one but leads to regrets and tearful nights in a pitch-black room where time is irreversible.

Ever since I lost my mom, I sealed the room for feelings and being emotionally attached to anyone. It was the best thing to do, perhaps for the best. That was when I tried going into a relationship with someone's daughter before healing. It was as if they had a picture of me in the house with them, but my soul and emotional attachments were below the river. My Ex once told me that it's ok to be emotional and open up your feelings. But what she failed to understand was that I didn't want a Lukewarm love; I desired a love so deep that could burn my lips and engulf my soul. While I was still a loner, I sometimes admired couples in love, but for some reason, I just knew I wasn't ready to be with anyone as of yet. I first learnt whom I was before telling someone else that I loved them. The greatest thing about loving yourself is that you get a chance to meet the real deal, which reflects your own self-love. You get an opportunity to study your motives, understand your likes your dislikes, and you also get a chance of a lifetime to connect with yourself. The satisfaction of Self-Discovery contrasts nicely with pain and suffering, which are both forms of feeling bad after a heartbreak or being punched to the throat by the school of Hard-Knocks. It's closely related to the value, desire and putting in work or the efforts you invest in seducing a woman or man before the insertion and thrusting of a penis into their vagina for sexual pleasure. Learn how to love yourself for as long as it takes because if you don't, you'll be stuck chasing people who won't love you either. Sometimes we long for relationships with imaginary people or materialistic things out of reach, and we forget to embrace or recognise what's around us. But if you pose for a second and look close enough, you will come to realise how much you have missed out all these years. Sometimes, your heart desires and needs aren't that far from you than you think. You have to recognise your worth and, once in a while, open your eyes wide open like a trader on the stock market looking for the best investment. Persistence, on the other hand, prevails. I once in a while drive to different places locally, and I sit down quietly to listen and observe what's around me. The experience only gives me a clear untold but personally seen pictures of how other people live differently from my life. From the eyewitness, most people are miserable, troubled to appoint that they walk home arguing with themselves. Whenever I gain insight into a complex situation or problem, I gain an accurate and deep understanding of it. Speaking of which? Whilst sitting in my car in the parking lot, a family of six parked their car right next to mine. And as they were making their way out of the car, a young boy aged four years old tapped twice onto her mother's shoulder on her way out of the vehicle, saying; "mom, mom, mom, mom."

"For God's sake! What?" Mom furiously responded because she was attending to the little sister who was screaming on top of her lungs because she wanted to be carried off the ground instead of the two-month-old baby. While her brother couldn't stop yapping either.

"You can't believe what I just saw while dad was driving us here." The little boy said.

"Of course, we won't unless you tell us." His dad responded.

"Mommmmmmmmmmmmmmmm! Can you imagine?" The boy added.

"Imagine what Dave?" The mom shouted.

"Mom, mom. I saw this old man with a young woman kissing. Yuks! Why would a young girl kiss such an old man in public? Or even be together in that case?" The little boy asked his mom.

"Well! First of all, it's not your business, and secondly; love doesn't ask why and neither has it been bothered with age. All that matters is as long as they're happy." The little boy's mom added.

"Hhhhmmmmmmm! So, if I came home with a grandma, you guys won't be furious about it?" The talkative boy asked his parents.

"Well! You're too young to be worried about love at the age of five." Dad responded again.

"We will see about that. I actually have a crush on my English teacher." The young boy replied while the little crying sister was repeatedly saying; "in your dreams Prince charming."

I looked at the two siblings while they walked off with their parents, and I wondered what a generation we are raising nowadays. Looking at them walking around as a disorganised family who couldn't agree with one another, and looking at myself being alone, functional and happy, left me wondering. However, much you feel sad about someone you have lost, beating down on yourself won't bring them back to life. One way or the other, we will all be called or vanish from the surface of the earth. Appreciate what you can hold onto right now and live life to the fullest. Cherish the little details, the small accomplishments, the moments you've collected for all these years as you collectively continue working on yourself. In most cases, when a relationship ends, the most loyal stay single until the wounds of heartbreak have partially healed. The other enters a new relationship before dawn because they can't stand the silence of being alone. They, therefore, don't hesitate to fill up that vacant position by looking for someone else because they don't know how to love themselves. And they are not patient enough to know how to wait for something special to come along naturally. They immediately look for who can fill up that missing void. In a nutshell, they go through life destroying hearts because of their emotional immaturity and lack of self-love that doesn't allow them to embrace and deal with loneliness. The first sign of lack of self-love is not knowing what you want in life and not having a clue of the person you're deep down. You can never love another soul; if you can't stand the person, you're. No wonder some couples date for ten years, but as soon as they get married, the friendship they endured for all those years vanishes and leads to divorce within less than a week of honeymoon. But strangers who have dunked on their first date are now celebrating their 15th anniversary. Some people get married after six months of knowing each other and are still happily married. A man who truly loves you doesn't need two years plus to see whether he needs to match you. If he genuinely loves you, he only needs a short period of months in. There is no formula to this. Do what makes you fucking happy. Love isn't about how many days, weeks or months you have known the person or been together. Spending good times together, it loves each other right, equally, noticing every single detail in someone and accepting them for who they're but not what you want them to be. When you have been through so much bullshit in life, sometimes being involved in something feels like an actual set-up. I guess that's why some people's online dating presence describe the traits they're looking for, such as someone who preferably can pay for luxurious travels and can buy you luxury items. But realistically, that someone who can feel your apartment with an attractively arranged bunch of flowers won't bring you peace because that isn't love. I might be rough around the edges, but I'm beyond blessed. How do I know that? The answer to that is pretty simple. Not many people appreciate themselves and learn how to love themselves either. The worst scenario is that those who desperately want to can't bear children, like many couples who have gone through a lot trying to make a child but have failed. Then you find the sad ones who give birth and dump them into pits, bins, toilets and entrances of fire stations. If my parents, who were poor at that time, managed to raise me, why wouldn't I be appreciative of the greatest gift to have happened to me, my children?

We sometimes listen to friends input on how life needs to be or the bad decisions we make, and we forget not everyone who offers an ear is an actual friend. I'm not telling you to become rebellious at everyone around you, but I want you to understand that some people we call friends are just counting for when you give up on what you have so they can take your place. The point is that self-love is a journey meant to be done by you and no one else. Don't ever let people guilt you into communicating with them. I don't speak to anyone that irritates me, and I give people no chances; if I feel like replying to a message three years later, then that's what I am going to do. Sometimes I ghost people just because I think they need to be paused for a bit or rejected out of my circle of life for the good of my soul. That may sound like I am being a dickhead, but I consider that as 'protecting my energy.' Considering the grave nature of what's happening to us, you must protect your energy level at all costs and always be ready for anything out of the ordinary at any given time. If the enemy is to attack, they don't wait for you to first have a cuppa. They do before you even take a shit. Don't tell the good news to people until it's manifested. You might question yourself or think of me as a crazy person for having said this. But the reality of things is that not everyone around you wants to see you shine. I understand we're not heaven-sent, but I would like you to also understand that not every bird that flocks together agrees with one another's ideas or celebrates each other's victory. Many people have friends they don't even know their last names or have never seen any of their family members. But just because they're afraid of being lonely or bored of themselves, they keep riding with the same person who adds no value to their life whatsoever. Have the courage to walk away from anything that doesn't bring you peace, anything that diverts you from your intended set goals, desires and aspirations. The fascinating thing about life is that; a small water bottle at the supermarket is worth £0.90. At a corner shop, it's £1.20. The same bottle at a five-star hotel is £3, and at Entebbe, Airport is 5,000 Ugandan Shillings and at Heathrow, Airport, London £5. Remember, this is the same bottle, same tasteless brand. The only thing that changes is the place where it's sold. Each location gives a different value to the same item. When you feel worthless, change places, don't stay there. Move and go somewhere you're appreciated because you're not a bloody tree. Have the courage to change your circle of influence and go to a place that sees your value. Surround yourself with people who appreciate your worth more than they praise you for the good things you do for them. Don't ever seek refuge in a circle, group of people, or someone else's life, especially if they make you feel like a worthless piece of S#*¶T.

Are Male Comedians Feminists?: When women behave in ways that don't fit their gender stereotype such as being assertive. They are viewed as less likeable and ultimately less hirable and that they're not wife material. Does that same hold true for men or they are straight-away penalized for straying from the strong masculine stereotype? Men too face backlash when they don't adhere to masculine gender stereotypes, especially when they show vulnerability, act nicer to society, display empathy, express sadness, exhibit modesty, and proclaim to be feminists. When it comes to showing vulnerability. Men are socialized to not ask for help or be vulnerable and they can be penalized when they challenge this notion. When a man asks for help, they are viewed as less competent, capable, and confident or treated less of a man. And when he makes themselves vulnerable by disclosing their weakness, they are perceived to have lower status. This is problematic, as not seeking help when you need it or admitting areas for improvement inevitably leads to mistakes and less development. In most cases women are shown empathy more than men, they're more likely to receive credit for being empathetic than men. You owe yourself the love you freely give to people who don't appreciate it or the ones that take you for granted. Don't kiss Ass or lick someone else's shoes so you can fit into a click of the group. I watched Dave Chappelle special with my girlfriend on Netflix to see what the media's fuss was about his stand-up comedy. He made some colour jokes about Covid-19; he made jokes about paedophilia and the reality of police brutality. Dave spoke of ageist and crude things, with politically incorrect metaphors about the Jewish Community and the Women's March. He made some coarse statements about trans phobia and how the LGBTQIA led to the death of his trans friend, whom he mentioned was an adorable and funny person. He mentioned a few names of people's lives that LGBTQIA has destroyed, and he kindly asked them to stop attacking people. Along with earnest statements about the LGBTQIA, the movement juxtaposes to hundred+ of years African Americans have been fighting for Equality. He mocked poor white people and joked about the irony of his journey with a transgender friend, whom he seemed emotionally upset about her death. I think it's time to change our ways because so many people are silently dying because of how we respond to the comments they make. It was my first-time watching Dave Chappelle's stand-up comedy, but to be perfectly honest.

We enjoyed every minute of his show. We laughed the roof off; we laughed all the way hysterically through the show because it was funny. He wasn't hateful of the LGBTQIA, and it was brash, sarcastic wit shared through a comic lens. However, his performance illustrated a peculiar irony in which most of us find ourselves imprisoned. Out of all the groups they comically and mercilessly joked about, only one group has decided to annihilate free speech over it. Not only are they never to be fooled about, but they can determine what group members can do so to view based on what they find funny. Isn't that ironic? It's not cool at all to cancel someone or even demonstrate hateful behaviours because a comment or joke they've made against your 'click of the group' doesn't seem to stand well with you or because the truth can't be tolerated. That doesn't seem like a group for equality, not even a single bit because that's somewhat biased. The world is watching and noticing every act, but the only problem with today's society is that they can't say shit about it because they're afraid of being cancelled. Look at how the world is today; the first thing we do when something bad happens or police brutality takes place, they rather take out cameras and start recording the incident, rather than stopping such hateful behaviours or helping someone from catching fire in a building or car that has been involved in an accident. Then when the government pulls upon them, they end up routing stores and burning history down to the ground. I guess! Watching too much TV has brainwashed many of us, and spending too much time reading filtered newspapers is the problem in today's society. People, especially those in developed countries, have been raised in fear, don't talk to a stranger, don't smile at a stranger that shit is dangerous. No wonder many people have closed mouths, tickets go higher yearly, and we all sit there quietly without questioning. But the economy and state of living are rapidly rising, and housing is soon becoming unaffordable for low-income earners. In developed countries, the pay raises should at least be fifteen pounds, considering how rates of everything else arise. People have grown and will always walk in fear and continue to be controlled like Jim Henson controlled his puppets.

This isn't an attack on the government or anyone in particular because it's the reality of things nowadays. In general, these are the same type of people who break the laws, but it becomes illegal when their followers do the same. Are they even aware of the number of times the government has been blamed for everything that happens to its citizens? I bet it's a lot more than what newspapers write about or hear on breaking news. And they still serve the same people blaming them; let's say they were to flip a switch on people's actions, we wouldn't be here. We would hate ourselves for it, and sooner or later, we would relocate to a forest where only crickets live and birds freely chip without being censored or judged by a group of people. People have matched with you in solidarity several times because they're fighting for equality and diversity to leave freely without the fear of being miss judged. So, when you get to sit at the high table, please don't use it aimlessly because you can and have the power to cancel everyone who makes a joke to make ends meet. Tell me! What is it called when a group of people attempt to dictate the production of pure art in an economy filled with misery and infections eating their guts out from every corner, based solely on their likes or dislikes and, by extension? The same group of people determines the cultural norms through inflicting fear and intimidation or else cancellation. Is that what we have become? Tell me otherwise because it's sickening to the guts. Or is that how we want to continue living? J.K. Rowling faced a backlash after tweeting her support for a woman with a history of making considered transphobic comments; "dress however you please. Call yourself whatever you like. Sleep with any consenting adult who will have you. Live your best life in peace and security. But force women out of their jobs for stating that sex is real?"

She then added the hashtags "#IStandWithMaya" and "ThisIsNotADrill," making it clear that she was referring to Maya Forstater, a British researcher who lost her job at a non-profit think tank following a series of tweets that were criticized as transphobic. Since then, some people want J.K. Rowling cancelled when she stood up for a woman with a history of questioning the legitimacy of trans identities. Two in five trans people have experienced a hate crime or incident, nearly half of trans people don't feel comfortable using public facilities for fear of harassment, and a third of trans people report being discriminated against because of their gender identity when visiting a bar or a restaurant in the past year. Many other artists have been cancelled in similar ways, and situations have led to self-ham. The world is fucked up after what we've all been through, so many things have changed in the process, and many people are still nursing wounds from the losses endured. Covid-19 has done enough damage, and if you haven't learnt from these past experiences caused by the pandemic, that's how you will die, selfish, closed-minded and ignorant. The thing is, you can't cancel someone willing to walk away from themselves because comedy has been here before a 'group of people came out of the closet, and it's still one of the few pure forms of arts left, so let's stop watching silently and let a ruling class corrupt it. People stop taking things personally and let artists make amends; we all have a choice to either watch it or completely ignore the person's comments or what's being said about us. If presidents shot everyone who made fun of them, the world would be out of breath. Streets would be breading, and the ghost of a monk would-be singing kumbaya. So, if you are the type that doesn't like people just for the sake of hate. Suppose you don't like something you can choose not to buy from me, or not watch what I have produced. Given there's a lot more production to choose from, both parties are happy. Close your eyes and pretend the producer you want to cancel doesn't exist, like we both don't exist on the surface of the earth. But what you and your click can't do is to take away someone's choice based on your inability to take a joke or a comment. Speaking of choices! Whist on the short holiday in Uganda, the pearl of Africa, a year of mixed emotions, just before the end of 2020, I spent an hour at the bank with the Oldman, as he had to deposit a chunk of money for a land title to be transferred in his name. I was supposed he asked me to come along, but I guess he was teaching me something indirectly. He has his ways, and not match of a talker, but rather a listener. We didn't say much on our way there, but while waiting to be served, I couldn't resist myself, and I asked him; "Oldman, why don't I activate your internet banking?"

"Why would I do that?" He asked with a serious facial expression.

"Well, then you won't have to spend an hour or so waiting in such a long queue to make simple banking transactions. Technology has long developed since the golden age error, that we can now even do shopping online, and so does banking. Your life will be so easy!" I enthusiastically added because I was so excited about initiating him into the world of online banking. "If I do that, I won't've to step out of the house?" He asked.

"Yes, yes"! I said, and I told him how even groceries can be delivered to his doorstep. The daredevil look he gave me, and his response left me tongue-tied.

"Since I entered this bank today, I have met four of my friends. I have chatted a while with the staff who know me very well by now. You know, ever since you guys grew up and all my friends died. I am all alone, and this is the company I need. I like to get ready and come to the bank. I have enough time because it's the physical touch that I crave. Two years back, I got sick. The store owner from whom I buy fruits came to see me and sat by my bedside and cried. When your mom fell a few days back while on her morning walk, our local grocer saw her and immediately got his car to rush her home as he knows where I live. Tell me! Would I have that human touch if everything evolved online?" He added.

"Why would I want everything delivered to me and force me to interact with just my computer?" He asked again and he added; I like to know the person I am dealing with and not just the 'seller'. Physical appearance creates a bond of relationships no technology can provide. Once again, tell me! Do these online services you talk about to deliver all the mentioned as well?"

"Son! Technology isn't the life for old folks like us, we like the physicality of others, the actual human to human connections and good customer service a human being can offer, we love chatting about our lives and talking about what we've been through and mentioning those that have passed. When you get to my age you will understand what I mean by this, but before then let me spend the time I have left with the people who make an impact in my life, but I won't choose to spend such priceless time with devices." The old man concluded.

His response left me speechless, and I couldn't argue with a statement that strong. I just shut my mouth and waited for him to finish his business. But I noticed something; there was this young at teller four he couldn't take his eyes off. He kept on allowing others to go ahead, and it took me a while to get it until I noticed she was the only one who was busy and as soon as she was free. The old man walked to the brownies counter. She was the reason he was constantly smiling while in the queue. They talked first for as much as it took her to transact his funds as instructed by the previous landowner. I remembered my little self as a child. The area I grew up in had beautiful shops and petrol station pump attendants who attracted several men to represent these businesses. But little did I know the aim behind it all. Driving down the road, I saw my ex. It's funny how "I would hit that" changes meaning over the years. She didn't see me because she didn't think I had a suck of balls to own a car. One of the lamest reasons she left was because I was poverty-stricken, and she was high maintenance. Yet she was coming from a church mouse broke type of family where they never owned a bicycle, but with an expensive taste who desired to live Beyonce's lifestyle. Without ambition and with no effort whatsoever to find a job but with an appetite to find a rich man. She left my broken ass with two of our children, and she ran off with a married man she previously dated before we met, and as of this day, they've two children together. She's the type of woman who doesn't even care about the children she pushed out of her womb ever since the married man rented her an apartment and informed her not to bring anyone around, not even her broke ass family members. The thing with married men and side dishes is that they promise to divorce their wives before they jump into your panties and whenever they're horny after being denied sex for weeks or months by their wives. They enjoy playing mind games with money-minded girl child's and vulnerable single women because they understand their weaknesses and know how desperate they can become. Side dishes have a saying; "we love the freedom of not having him around, to monitor our whereabouts all the time."

Yet the 'I desperately want a husband of my own' are easily manipulated by married men because of their weakness to wants. It shouldn't be a crime to want something of your own, but it also wouldn't have killed you if you focussed on loving the miserable person, you are. She, on the other hand, needs much more support than what you seek out. When you meet someone with good intentions, it feels just like coming across good customer service; you might unintentionally buy the entire stock of their goods. I love travelling to new places and meeting new people. You learn new things from them, and you see many surprising things you wouldn't be able to see in your room by staring at your ceiling for hours. Whilst approaching the festive sessions in mid-October, I boarded a plane from London Heathrow to Uganda that was passing via Amsterdam. During his introduction, the pilot made everyone laugh; he said; "ladies and gentlemen welcome aboard. This is your captain speaking. This journey to Amsterdam will take approximately forty-five minutes. So, you have those minutes to do whatever you want and if you're someone who's on a mission to find you a love nest. Now it's your chance to engage with strangers from different destinations or catch up with someone from previous passings. You can ever meet new ones and mingle. I know for a fact that your all grown-ups, so do whatever the heck you want, but don't let time pass you by."

Some people can be so toxic to your health. They can't afford to love you right; they don't want to let you go, and they don't want you to find someone else. The more you give, the less they appreciate, and the minute you have had enough and decide to walk away is when they are ready to love and treat you right. So, you give them a chance hoping they have changed, only to realize they're still the fake ass manipulative, self-centred and controlling scumbags. You find the strength to walk away once more, and here they come again proclaiming their love for you, and you give in, again. Someone showing anger and persistence to get you back once you try to break it off isn't proof of love; it's a knee jerk reaction. Someone kissing your ass or making flaccid attempts to be nicer for a short period of time isn't proof that they are trying to rebuild what's broken. It's proof that they adequately understand you, to know how to defuse you long enough and hook you once again. Take away a toy; a little boy cries, take away a relationship of convenience, a grown-ass man cries as he did as a child with his toys. Just because he cries doesn't mean you give him what he wants. Stop listening to what that person keeps promising and start watching what their actions actually keep telling you. A lot of you women don't know what it's like to be loved by a real man. You know lust, you know joy, you know the passion, and you know the fear of abandonment. But they end up encountering love bombing, which happens when someone overwhelms you with loving words, submissive actions, and behaviour as a manipulation technique. It's often used to win over your trust and affection so that they can meet a goal of theirs. Love bombing can also be used for either positive or negative purposes, which can as well begin a cycle of abuse where the love bomber withholds love and attention to manipulate you. Being showered with love can feel so good! It can be an instant confidence boost to feel wanted and appreciated by someone. However, dating a love bomber isn't going to look the same in every situation. Still, a few telltale signs of a love-bombing partner are extravagant gifts, obsessive flattery, constant complimentary texting, and always expecting a prompt reply. If you have been in a relationship with someone with narcissistic traits, you may relate to the narcissistic abuse cycle that involves love bombing. Narcissistic traits involve grandiosity, lack of empathy, and a need for admiration to regulate a fragile sense of self and low self-esteem. Narcissistic love bombing is in the abusive cycle, which can be recognized easy if you start experiencing signs of love bombing so that you can avoid getting stuck in the abuse cycle. This narcissistic personality disorder often develops from some form of abuse or neglect in early childhood development. Modelling of proper self-soothing or socialization didn't happen for the afflicted person. Due to the individual with narcissistic personality disorder's intense need to regulate their self-esteem ignore their partner's boundaries in the relationship in favour of their needs. The person tends to crave control of their partner to regulate their self-esteem best. Typically, control is achieved through the love bombing cycle of abuse. There are many more signs to look out for, such as how that person compliments you. Do they use their loved ones 'family and friends? Does the pacing of the relationship make sense?

Do they feel like they are somewhat about themselves? Case in point, that dress I bought you looks good on you; I have excellent taste, huh!? Do they have a high sense of grandeur, seeming full of themselves without much to back it up? Are they short-tempered or frequently become overly angry? Does this person seem possessive and checks in all the time but frames it that they are doing it for your safety?

On a second note, not all partners sending you love letters and flowers are narcissistically love bombing you. And when your partner makes a mistake, try not to think of them as bad people or classify them as your EXs. Love bombing is a narcissistic abuse cycle often associated with the abuser having a narcissistic personality disorder. Think back to some of the red flags above. In a healthy relationship, both partners will consent to the pace. Love will build over time as you learn about and accept each other's strengths and flaws. When in a healthy relationship, you will feel equal respect, trust, and honesty. You will enjoy spending time away from each other because your choices are mutual, and each person feels like an equal partner. In contrast, there is typically an imbalance of power in an unhealthy relationship. One of the partners may feel entitled to overstep the other person's boundaries in the abuse cycle. It would be best if you never gave up your sense of physical or emotional safety and security for someone else's comfort. You don't have to ignore your boundaries and needs in favour of someone else's. No rationale makes that okay. Even if you think you are helping the person, you may be giving them the message that their actions are okay. A relationship should be mutually satisfying. Be sure to check in with your feelings regularly. If you find yourself worrying about your partner's happiness more than your own, then do some reflecting. Once you have reflected, try to restore a sense of balance by setting boundaries. Gauge your partner's reactions to your limitations or expectations. If your partner tries to intimidate you into a power imbalance, then it may be time for you to move on. Love shouldn't hurt; it should feel comfortable in your partner's arms, being yourself around that person and accepting you for who you are deep inside. Stop chasing your idea of what love should be and recognise what love is. Love isn't promising to act right after he gets caught fucking up time and time again. Love is him acting right from the start because he doesn't want to fuck up. Love isn't telling your grown-ass man that he needs to change so he can keep you; love is when that grown ass man changes from bad behaviour to become a devoted husband or partner you once fell ears for, on his own because he can't imagine life without you. On the other hand, not all partners are the same, think the same way, act or even behave the same way as we think they do. Men don't tend to hate their EXs as women do after a break-up. Some men abandon their children in previous relationships not because they don't love their kids or are deadbeats the way media chose to categorise all baby daddies.

Don't get me wrong, we have deadbeats out there, but it might as well be because the new women they meet see a father's relationship with his children as red flags. Deadbeat is a pejorative term referring to parents who don't fulfil their parental responsibilities, especially when they don't want anything to do with the pregnancy or child's life, they even evade court-ordered child support obligations or custody arrangements. They are also referred to as absentee fathers and mothers. they do not treat their children with respect as individuals. They won't compromise, take responsibility for their behaviours, or apologize. Often these parents have a mental disorder or a serious addiction. We may all live with the consequences of poor parenting. However, if your childhood was traumatic, you might carry wounds from abusive or dysfunctional parenting. When they haven't healed, toxic parents can re-injure you in ways that make growth and recovery difficult. When you grow up with dysfunctional parenting, you may not recognize it as such. It feels familiar and normal. We may be in denial and not realize that we've been abused emotionally, particularly if our material needs were met. Sometimes, it's impossible to hold on to healthy behaviours when we are around our parents. Our boundaries were learned in our family. If we don't go along, our family, especially parents, may test us. You may have trouble setting new boundaries with your parents. Perhaps you have a mom who calls every day or a sibling who wants to borrow money or is abusing drugs. Confused, they may attack you or blame your new limits on your partner. Holding healthy relationships with deadbeat parents can be hard to walk away from. You may need distance from your parents to create the boundaries that you're unable to make verbally. But what really drives some males to be deadbeat dads?

It's because of the sexist double standard regarding the value of parenthood when it comes to males. this is most evident in the frequent political rhetoric of the sexist/feminist left, as they often refer to the (mostly economic) sympathy we should be extending to the single mom. In doing so they create a protected class, which is all fine and good were it not for their complete denial of the other party to the child's existence; the party that has no right to choose, the party who post-intercourse becomes a parent whether they like it or not. no right to choose but 50-100% of the financial obligations. it is often this financial obligation that prevents divorced fathers from actually being fathers at all. may I remind everyone in this society, that for every "single mom", there is a "single dad" who in most cases should be granted equal protected status, but who is rarely extended the slightest consideration either incorporate society or within the legal community and court system? For clarification, I am not referring to the first few months or even a year or two of life, but the remaining, equally important next years. My argument points out that the very term deadbeat dad supports a sexist notion and fails to illuminate the big picture. Deadbeat dads are the by-product of a morally deficient societal code and the court system that fails to acknowledge a man's right to fatherhood once a woman chooses to bear his offspring, not solely as our sexist feminist culture would have it as an obligation with a variety of reasons you can think of. Some men never wanted to become fathers in the first place, because they believe the pregnancy was accidental. This type of man tries his best to pretend he's not because he hates the mother of the child who ate his abortion monies and kept the pregnancy a secret. This man doesn't want to think about the offspring that may or may not be his. The media doesn't specify between the two differences of men where some fathers are in the latter category, who really wanted to be in the child's life, but every time they find where they live, the child's mother decides to move and run from someone who has paid child support as often as he saw the child(ren) until his death.

Now! This is a man who wanted to become a father so

bad, but he wasn't given a chance to prove themselves or allowed to be, so holds onto the money as leverage to be allowed to be the father to his child(ren) the way he wants things to be. A deadbeat dad is a political word in order to force fathers to pay child support payments. You either make your payments or get dehumanized as a deadbeat dad and no one will ever talk with you. Here is the cost of being a deadbeat dad: You go to jail, your credit is ruined, you lose access to your kids. So here is another way to ask the question: Why would someone normal choose to go to jail, ruin their credit, and lose access to their kids? The answer to that question is that rational people don't do that. Rational people make the payments, pay the money not go to jail or destroy their credit. We need to stop dehumanizing words until we understand the problem. The media needs to deep-dive the studies of what a deadbeat parent is. We live in a world where women are the ones that sometimes have to make child support payments 15% of the time. So, we need to understand this population of men and women and try to figure out why this is occurring. No one benefits from short term solution that basically dehumanizes people in order to get them to do something. It doesn't help the kids or any member of the family or society. We need a better approach. Do we really take time to ask why there are more deadbeat fathers than deadbeat mothers?

In most family cases we hear, mothers are usually automatically given custody because of the simple fact that they are mothers. Even if they are bad mothers, it is very difficult for a father to gain custody of a child(ren) because many judges believe that it will negatively affect the child(ren) if you remove them from their mother's custody. They believe it is the natural order of things. The media doesn't show us that side of these amazing fathers out there who fight for custody to protect their children and lose simply because they are men, armed with ample evidence of neglect, and many other things which don't really matter. Looking at the street every evening, homelessness would be one factor; the high male incarceration rate would be another. Furthermore, as women are almost always awarded custody in family courts, regardless of the woman's ability to care for the child(ren) the legal system more often puts men in a position that will put them in jeopardy of not being able to pay the court-mandated payments. It would be interesting to see the stats on what percentage of women have been ordered to pay child support that is delinquent on their payments and considered deadbeat moms.

Some people are cut off from family for that reason or due to unresolved anger and resentment from childhood. Cut-offs may be necessary for very abusive environments. However, although they reduce emotional tension, the underlying problems remain and can affect all of your relationships. The ideal way to become independent from your family is to work on yourself, then go to your parents and practice what you have learned. It's far better for your growth to learn how to respond to domestic abuse. I have witnessed friends who felt uncomfortable returning home do this. They gradually transitioned from reluctantly staying in their parents' residence during home visits, to becoming comfortable declining invitations home, to staying in a hotel or with friends without guilt. Some could eventually stay with their parents and enjoy it. We sometimes blame our parents for not being able to give us all we thought we could've had as children and we forget our parents sacrificed a lot for us to be. You will never understand that being a parent is being completely selfless. Until when you have you have your own children, then you will acknowledge that becoming a parent means putting the needs of your children before your own. This comes in every aspect, from money to poor sleeping patterns, to letting their friends down, to cancelling long-term plans and literally everything is affected by this beautiful new lifestyle. And that is easier to do when you see this precious and helpless newborn baby that you both created. However, as the baby grows some dads and sometimes moms want to do their own thing. Being a parent is a twenty-four-seven demanding unpaid job, it's too much commitment, is just too much, and so much more than they are willing to do. Live alone outnumbered hidden agendas such bankruptcy, poor sex, bad connections, horrible kissers, low voltage of chemistry between. But parental responsibility might be one of the main reasons to why most couples break up after childbirth.

What the media doesn't clarify is the type of father who might unintentionally abandon you as a child because your mom told them to fuck off, and disappear not to contact them again. Or in most cases when the mother wants to control the children's custody and life in general. Because she's still in denial about the separation, and she has done everything in her power to assemble their broken relationship. Still, the man has had enough, and he doesn't want anything to do with the EX other than maintaining a solid connection with his children. The woman then decides to refuse him shared custody but allows him to come to her house because she believes it's the only safe place, he can be able to see his own children. Which sometimes tends to be a cheese trap for catching a mouse. Some women lose out on good connections while busy chasing the bad influences, and they regret the good opportunities they missed when it's too late. Some people will never know how lucky and blessed they're because they pray to God to help them find someone special. But as soon as they find that person who treats them better than all EXs combined, they start playing games and being dramatic. While out and about, they seem like they're still searching for more than what they have. The point is exact; when a genuine man approaches you for the first time and shows interest more than five times, but you are playing for keeps or had to be caught by telling him how it's not going to be possible for the two of you to happen. Honey, once that interested man walks out of desire, count him gone. Men are built to want things and then go after what they want that instant, but once what they go for or show interest in doesn't correspond well with their desire, men tend to give up easily. In simple terms, let go and move on until they stumble into someone else who seems interested. Men attend to women for two reasons, sex and love, but in most cases, men do not marry for sex or love; they marry for stability. A man can Love you and not marry you. A man can have sex with you for years without marrying you. But he immediately finds someone who brings stability to his life; he marries her. What I mean by stability is 'Peace of Mind' I have heard some men making such a statement 'I love this lady, but I don't think I can spend the rest of my life with her.' Men are visionaries when they think about marriage; they don't think about wedding dresses, bridesmaids, anything that most Ladies thinks is fanciful. Men aren't as demanding as women are but they will think to themselves, can she give me peace of mind? Will she be able to build with me? Can this woman build me a home? Can she take care of my children and me? Can this woman be supportive of my goals?

Men don't like a woman who gives them discomfort, and this is why a man can stay with a woman for years and meet another in a month, then get married to her. it's not because the woman has aged; it's the comfort of having peace of mind we men want. sex is a pleasure, love is an affection, respect, on the other hand, is stability for a man, and it doesn't matter how much he earns. the worst prison for a man is a home without peace of mind or the one where security is tighter than a cowboy ashore in tight pants. men tend to question everything they see but don't like to be questioned, something I can't explain as to why it's the way it is. so, you have got to be careful whom you give your heart to, fall in love with or marry. if he's interested in you with good intentions, give that man a chance, he won't blow it like a candle on a birthday cake. Give the man a chance because there's no harm in trying. Otherwise, how will you know if he loves you if you don't give him a chance to prove his intentions towards you? But if you undoubtedly know, you are not interested in that man. Just stop wasting his time and eating his money or cancel the booty calls with him whenever you feel the need to fuck. I know it's a lot to take in and think about. But we both want the same thing, to be loved the same way we pour love onto others. Like my late granddad, peace be upon him, used to say; 'the only fly which cares is the one that flies onto your wound to suck pus out of it to heal.' After having gone through traumatising events or having escaped an abusive relationship, the man you meet today isn't the enemy who caused damage in your past life. All he wants is to love you right and perhaps make things right with your past. Have you noticed the only bird that dares to peck an eagle is a raven?

He sits on his back and bites his neck. However, the eagle does not respond nor fight with the raven; it does not spend time or energy on the raven. The eagle just opens its wings and rise higher because the higher the flight, the harder it is for the raven to breathe, and then the raven falls due to lack of oxygen. The point is, stop wasting time with the ravens, just take them to your heights, and they will fade away. Remember not to spend your precious time worrying about the foolishness of folks. Sometimes we don't see things for the way they're but how we want them to be. You shouldn't have to teach someone to love you, instead teach them how to treat you right. Forgive those who don't know how to love or treat you and consider the experience as a moment in which they were teaching you how to love yourself. Some men are looking for Queens that know how to be respectful and know-how to carry themselves in public as well as at home. Again, it doesn't matter what type of job he does or how much he brings to the table. Some men want to feel like they are in charge and respected as the head of the house. Don't get me wrong! Not all men deserve to be respected because some women are in relationships or married to scumbags, the jobless who are unbothered to even search for a job on the internet. Some men are drunkards who spend every penny earned at the pub, and some are domestic abusers. But what fascinates me to this day are the women who choose to stay with these dangerous, abusive animals, even after when the last borne in their body is broken or face bruised to a point, they are unrecognisable. Remember, respect is earned, not asked for or demanded that matter, and it should come from both sides. A real woman is slow to take but quick to show compassion and love towards the man she's really into. She loves genuinely by doing the unexpected simple things because she knows men like to feel special. People often think men don't have feelings because they are expected to be tough no matter what's thrown at them or show less of their emotional side not to appear weak to the public. Unfortunately, they do have a feeble emotional side and actual feelings. If you treat them right, they would be like little teddy bears who would love on you just as much as you love them. Some men intentionally hide their emotional side and feeling in many ways, such as being defensive or trying to avoid specific questions or situations, because they think by revealing that other part of who they are, women might see them as weak individuals.

So am challenging you to do something nice for your man for two weeks nonstop and watch how he will start acting right towards you. They will treat you like they should because they would like to know whether your connection isn't based on his money and possessions but the love and relationships, they want to develop in between. You will be surprised to know that some men like the same things as women, like seeking attention. If I were you reading this and it somehow relates, you would stop fussing as it's a total turn off. Might he be planning to do something special for you or about to set the mood right or going to fuck your brains out as the best sex you've ever had, and you ruin the mood with unnecessary fussing. That's not the best way to speak to your man if you are not happy about something or not feeling well for that matter is to say what's on your mind in a polite way possible. You are not responsible for the programming you received in childhood, and you are not to be blamed for your upbringing. That wasn't your job then; it was your parents' responsibility. But you are 100% responsible for fixing it as an adult. The mom who raised us could spit onto the ground expecting you to be back before the sand absorbed the saliva. My parents were strategically smart when it came to matters of discipline. No wonder we grew up so disciplined and unlike today's generation. Whenever I was sent to the shops, I went singing what I was told to buy, not to forget what it was in case I was distracted on the way. If you had to go back and ask what it was again, she could slap the stupidity out of me. The slap wasn't any slaps you could wish to receive from your parents. Like one of them used to say: "I will slap you and you see white forks."

Growing up, my parents beat me whenever I was naughty. Not to generalise, but I think most children from my and preceding generations of ass-whooping. When it comes to ass whopping, my parents would just surprise you by using anything around them. They would sneak up on you talking nicely and then use a belt or shoe on you the next minute. For most transgressions, I got an ass whooping to deter me from repeating the same thing. The whoopings varied in instruments used, geographical location of the said ass whooping and degrees of intensity. Looking back, I realise that some of the things my folks did during the process of whooping my ass were hilarious. I do not know if any of you can relate. The beatings were always in tune. When my dad and Mom would whoop me, the beatings were always rhythmic, accompanied by a message. Mostly, the message would be one that reminded me that she had told me several times not to do whatever it was I did. The strokes were periodical like every two seconds, a whooping would land if the situation was dire; if not, perhaps every five seconds. For every stroke that landed, words would be uttered. I-told-you-several-times-to-be-at-home-by-sun-set would be thirteen corresponding strokes. I had to get my own switch or belt that would be used to whoop my ass. There were two or three particular belts that were predominantly used for whooping. Mom or Dad or whomever the ass whooper was because there were many with the license Leather Belt to whoop. He would hold both ends together, making a loop on one end which would be the part that landed on my behind. The ceremonious switch was always from some fruit tree like a peach tree or a guava tree, we had fruit trees everywhere in my childhood home. The whooping would last for as long as the switch was useable. So, I had to be strategic when I got my switch. If I got a small switch, she would go out and get a bigger one, which would increase the intensity of the whooping. But I also didn't want to get a big switch because the whooping would last too long. It had to be just right, to be fair to my ass and my whooper's intention. Talk about being caught between a rock and a hard place. If I cried while getting my ass whooped, I would be told to keep quiet, with the threat of more whooping if I continued crying. It didn't matter how much it hurt. And if my whooper were really mad, I would be told to stop whimpering too. Which was hard to do after a good whooping? The pre-whooping phase was when I knew a whooping was imminent and a very uncertain place. My whooper would ask a question, my folks liked to engage in gaining understanding, or so he said. When I replied, he'd be like; "you are talking back to me? Do you think you are my peer? You think you're my size? And when I didnt answer to his questions, he would be like; "respond this instant!"

Both scenarios would dramatically increase the intensity of the whooping. Damned if you do, damned if you don't. The license to whoop was extended to teachers. During parent's day, my folks would strongly encourage my teachers to whoop my ass till I got onto the right path. And that, all my primary school teachers had bendable bamboo sticks, and boy was, these sticks active. If ever I got home and somehow it leaked that any teacher had whooped my ass for being naughty, additional whoopings were in order from my folks. There was no safe place! I am lucky and blessed to have been raised by strict parents. Everything I did or was told to do was timed, supervised for approval and monitored until everything was done right. But little did I know my folks were moulding me into who I am today. My childhood ass-whooping doesn't mean I should as well punish my children the same way. I have to do better than that because if you want to see good happening in your children's lives, you have to be able to do good deeds. Stop being controlled by the fear of what happened to you as a child. Stop waiting for someone special, but instead, make the one you have to be that special someone you seek. Learn to appreciate the little things you possess and give back the same love you wish to receive from your husband, wife or partner. There's no ideal man or woman out there unless you live in a fairytale story. I remember my late best friend Meddie asked me once; "who is your ideal woman."

"When you reach a certain age like I am. It's mostly about being loved right, respected, and teamwork. It's not just about having someone to have sex with but someone to share thoughts with and build together." I responded.

When you have lost good people around you, especially

a loved one, the reality behind grieving is that the pain never goes away, and as you get older. All you truly want is to be surrounded by good people with the same purpose and those who have been through the same situation as you. I am talking about the kind of people who are good to you and good for your soul. Some people can be beautiful on the outside but ugly on the inside. Usually, life takes more than it gives, but today life has granted you a chance to breathe. Use the time you have left on this earth wisely. I stopped sending paragraphs, stopped begging, quit telling people how to treat me, and started walking away, ignoring bullshit conversations, blocking useless connections and distancing myself from anyone who doesn't serve my purpose. Life-mate is lonely, but it's becoming peaceful. Sometimes being alone in life is better than being surrounded by half-ass people, orgasm fakers, and dishonesty. You have to fight for what you believe in and strive as much as you can and for as long as you're breathing, and whenever you are having a shitty day ahead of you, I want you to know that some of the best days in your life are coming. Because no matter the stormy weather, it eventually gets better, without any sort of explanation; one day, you realise that you're no longer upset nor mad, hurt or bothered by the things that took so much of your energy and thoughts. You will find yourself in a peaceful place and enjoy that feeling of having to wake up, and you don't have to be questioned about anything stupid. Losing a loved one is earth-shattering. If you support someone going through or recovering from trauma, remember that each person heals at their own pace. You can't control how they feel or tell them to stop grieving; that's not a choice you should make for them. You can be there by being an active listener. Give them space to talk about what they have been through, and respond with empathy, respect, compassion, and patience. Be honest about how you can provide support and help them seek out a professional when needed.

Connections involve emotional proximity, vulnerability, and intimacy. Events leading to trauma in a relationship may be recurring, making healing complex. It can help create boundaries for yourself during healing, connect with trusted individuals, and find a safe environment. It's also important to understand that grief is not a single emotion; it's an experience or state of being that manifests itself physically, emotionally, mentally, and spiritually following a painful or traumatic event. Moreover, like our fingerprints, each of us is unique. How we experience the loss of a loved one and how long we grieve can vary considerably following similar loss situations, such as the death of a parent, spouse, child, pet. That said, even though everyone experiences grief, there is a difference between the ordinary, uncomplicated, straightforward, abnormal, problematic, or exaggerated ways we respond to a personally painful or traumatic event. Given we all experiences grief in our way, most survivors usually exhibit some of these characteristics temporarily when responding to a loss in the days, weeks, or months after the death of a loved one; tears, crying or sobbing, an overall lack of energy, sleep pattern changes from too little or too much sleep, feeling indifferent about the day's necessary tasks or life in general. Changes in appetite, such as not feeling like consuming too much food, withdrawing from normal/usual social interactions and relationships. difficulty focusing on a task, whether at work, personally, a hobby, questioning spiritual or religious beliefs, job/career choices, or life goals. Feelings of anger, guilt, loneliness, depression, emptiness, sadness, but still occasionally experiencing moments of joy or happiness. Most grievers experience some or all of these reactions most profoundly in the immediate days following a loss but unhurriedly return to a new normal afterwards. You won't entirely forget your loved ones as if they never existed, but in time, you will learn how to cope with their absence and the scar on your heart and soul. Some people, however, might experience complicated grief in which the usual responses to the death of a loved one do not fade over time and can impair or prevent them from leading their everyday lives. Regardless of the phrasing, the characteristics of grief can include any of the symptoms above; anger, irritation, or episodes of rage, problems accepting the reality of the death, self-destructive behaviour, such as alcohol or drug abuse, an inability to focus on anything but the death of a loved one.

Focusing intensely on reminders of the deceased or excessive avoidance of such reminders. Intense feelings of sadness, pain, detachment, sorrow, hopelessness, emptiness, low self-esteem, bitterness. Longing for the deceased's presence and listening to the voice notes they last left you the day you didn't pick up the phone because you were busy trying to avoid them or the times you thought about them as a nuisance. As mentioned earlier, everyone's grief response is unique, and no specific amount of time defines when normal grief becomes complicated. Some impose a threshold of around six months after the death occurred. But it is perfectly normal for grievers to find the first year following a significant loss difficult as survivors experience holidays, birthdays, anniversaries, and other critical annual events for the first time without their loved ones. If you exhibit some of the characteristics of complicated grief above, still feel trapped in your grief and that your grief response remains the same or has intensified despite the passage of several months or more. Your cultural background can also affect how you understand and approach the grief process. Some cultures anticipate a time to grieve and have developed rituals to help people through the grief process. Grief rituals and ceremonies acknowledge the pain of loss while also offering social support and a reaffirmation of life. You may not be aware of how your own cultural background affects your grief process. Talking with family, friends or clergy is one way to strengthen your awareness of possible cultural influences in your life. Friends and family may be able to help you generate ideas to create your own rituals. Some have found solace in creating their own unconventional ceremonies, such as a funeral or ceremony with personal friends in a private setting. You might consider seeking help from a mental health professional. You should also consider joining a bereavement support group in your area, mainly if one exists for people who have experienced a similar type of loss of a spouse or parent. Grief typically causes feelings of isolation but discussing your situation with others mourning a death might help you gain a different perspective on your specific response. Letting go is problematic because it's normal to have difficulty recovering from trauma or pain from the past. Just because the experience is over doesn't mean you haven't been deeply affected. It can take time to recognize and understand what's happened and what it means for you. Letting go implies that we are releasing ourselves from parts of the past. This can be challenging when we've created bonds or have meaningful memories attached to the people we've lost, the places we have travelled, and the essential things we've accomplished or done with the deceased. We, the grievers, also have a hard time with change. Taking in or making sense of situations that affect how we see ourselves and the world is a complex task. Grief is one of those experiences you can never fully understand until you actually experience it, and, until that time, all a person has to go on is what they have observed and what they have been told. I can't put into words the grief that had beset me. But if it wasn't for me to discover how self-love is the soul's goal. Whatever your loss, it's personal to you, so please don't feel ashamed about how you think or believe that it's somehow only appropriate to grieve for certain things. If the person, animal, relationship, or situation was significant to you, it's normal to suffer the loss you are experiencing. Whatever the cause of your grief, though, there are healthy ways to cope with the pain that, in time, can ease your sadness and help you come to terms with your loss, find new meaning, and eventually move on with your life. When that wave of grief knocks you over, you want to know, "When will this end?"

All the things you have heard about getting over grief, going back to normal, and moving on are misrepresentations of what it means to love someone you have lost. I'm sorry, I know we humans appreciate things like closure and decisiveness, but this isn't how grief goes. In fact, there is a very small proportion of people might have what we now call extended grief disorder. Something we start looking for after six months or a year after a death or loss, and what we see, in such cases, is that this person has not been able to function day to day the way that they wish that they could. They are not getting out the door to work or getting dinner on the table for their kids, or they're not able to, say, listen to music because it's just too upsetting. When you care for someone going through this terrible process of losing someone, it really is more about listening to them and seeing where they are at in their learning than trying to make them feel better. The point is not to cheer them up. The point is to be with them and let them know that you will be with them and that you can imagine a future for them where the waves of grief are not constantly knocking them over. You don't recover from grieve; however, not recovering from grief doesn't doom you to a life of despair. You will be surprised to hear that there are outnumbered people out there living normal and purposeful lives while also experiencing endless sorrow. This isn't to say that recovery doesn't have a place in the grieving process. It's simply what we are recovering from that needs to be redefined. To heal means to return to a normal state of health, mind, or strength, and as many would attest, when someone very significant dies, we never return to a pre-loss normal. The loss, the person who died, our grief all get integrated into our lives, and they profoundly change how we live and experience the world.

Ongoing grief is normal, not dysfunctional. It's also not dysfunctional to experience unpleasant grief-related thoughts and emotions from time to time, sometimes even years later. We're meant to experience both sides of the emotional spectrum, not just the warm and half fuzzy. As grieving people, this is especially true. Where there are things like love, appreciation, and fond memory, there will also be sadness, yearning, and pain. And though these experiences seem in opposition to one another, we can experience them all simultaneously. People may push you to stop feeling the pain, but this is misguided. If the pain always exists, it makes sense because there will never come a day when you won't wish for one more moment, one more conversation, one last hello, or one final goodbye. You learn to live with these wishes, and you learn to accept that they won't come true, not here on Earth, but you still wish for them. Experiencing pain doesn't contradict the healing potential. With constructive coping and maybe a little support, the intensity of your distress will lessen, and your recovery will evolve over time. Though there will be many ups and downs, you should, d eventually reach a place where you're having just as many good days as bad and then perhaps more good days than bad until one day you may find that your lousy grief days are few and far between.

Coming to terms: We don't recover from grief after losing a loved one because it's born when a loved one dies. And as long as that person remains, significant grief will stay. What will, hopefully, return to a general baseline is the level of intense emotion, stress, and distress that a person experienced in the weeks and months following their loss. So perhaps we recover from the extreme pain of grief, but we don't recover from the grief itself. But the grief, it's always there, like an old injury that aches when it rains. And though this prospect may be scary in the early days of grief, in time, you will find that you wouldn't have it any other way. Grief is an expression of love; these things grow from the same seed. Grief becomes a part of how we love despite someone's physical absence. It helps you connect to your memories from past experiences; and, therefore, bonds you with others through your shared humanity. And it provides you with a perspective on your immense ability for discovering strength and perspicuity in the most difficult of times. That said, it is a mistake to think that all painful experiences can and should be gotten over. When such a shift isn't possible, people can't always change how they think, feel, and behave simply because they want to. It's common to believe that, in these instances, one can go to therapy or take medication and be cured of these problems. Still, many people who have experienced things like severe hardship, trauma, addiction, and psychological disorder will tell you that healing isn't about putting these experiences in the past. Instead, it's about changing their relationship to the related thoughts, memories, behaviours, and emotions that exist in the present.

Sometimes, getting over something or forgetting isn't even desirable, such as getting over or forgetting about a deceased loved one and their ongoing absence. Still, many people mistakenly think that grief can and should end at some point. Those who understand grief in hindsight may believe this is a foolish mistake, but I would argue it's familiar and understandable, considering how little people know about grief before experiencing it. Especially those who live in societies where people are quick to believe that grief runs a linear and finite course and, consequently, encourage grieving people to push forward and let the woes of the past disappear like water under the bridge. The reality of grief is that it often stays with you until the day you, yourself, die. For those who think of grief as a negative emotion, I can see where this may seem unmanageable, but rest assured, the impact of grief changes over time. As you change your relationship with grief by changing how you respond to, cope with, and conceptualize grief, you will likely also find hope and healing. If you think about it, grief is one instance where there is a tangible benefit to accepting its ongoing presence in your life. Doing so creates more room for comfort, positive memories, and a constant connection with the person who died. I understand this progression because I have experienced it, but I'm sure it can be difficult to believe if you haven't. Initially, grief is unique, and relationships are special, so your relationship with grief and with the person who died will evolve in a complex and nuanced way. So, instead of generalizing and categorizing, embrace it, learn how to leave with it and embrace it because grief is a never-ending journey. Whatever your relationship with the person who died, it's important to remember that we all grieve in different ways. There's no single way to react.

When you lose someone important in your life, it's okay to feel how you feel. Some people express their pain by crying, others never shed a tear, but that doesn't mean they feel the loss any less. Don't judge yourself, thinking that you should be behaving in a different way, or try to impose a timetable on your grief. Grieving someone's death takes time. For some people, that time is measured in weeks or months, for others, it's in years. Allow yourself to feel the pain of loss as it pours down on you. The bereavement and mourning process can trigger many intense and unexpected emotions. But the pain of your grief won't go away faster if you ignore it. In fact, trying to do so may only make things worse in the long run. To eventually find a way to come to terms with your loss, you'll need to actively face the pain. Grief doesn't always move through stages, as you may have read in the previous paragraphs about the 'stages of grief' which are usually denial, anger, bargaining, depression, and acceptance. It all depends on the kind of grieving one is facing and how strong one is and given that we all experience grief in different ways, such as losing a job, losing a loved one, losing a pet, and a valuable object. However, many people find that grief following the death of a loved one isn't nearly that predictable. For some, grief can come in waves or feel more like an emotional rollercoaster. For others, it can move through some stages but not others. Don't think that you should be feeling a certain way at a certain time. Some days the pain of your bereavement may seem more manageable than others. Then a reminder such as a photo, a piece of music, or a simple memory can trigger a wave of painful emotions again. While you can't plan ahead for such reminders, you can be prepared for an upcoming holiday, anniversary, or birthday that may reignite your grief. Talk to other friends and family ahead of time and agree on the best ways to mark such occasions. Remember, the only cure for grief is to continue grieving and moving on doesn't mean forgetting your loved one. Finding a way to continue forward with your life doesn't mean your pain will end or your loved one will be forgotten.

Most of us carry our losses with us throughout life; they become part of who we are. The pain should gradually become easier to bear, but the memories and the love you had for the person will always remain. When you lose someone, you love, it's normal to want to cut yourself off from others and retreat into your shell. But this is no time to be alone. Even when you don't feel able to talk about your loss, simply being around other people who care about you can provide comfort and help ease the burden of bereavement. Reaching out to those who care about you can also be an important first step on the road to healing. While some friends and relatives may be uncomfortable with your grief, plenty of others will be eager to lend support. Talking about your thoughts and feelings won't make you a burden. Rather, it can help you make sense of your loved one's death and find ways to honour their memory. Lean on friends and family. Even those closest to you can struggle to know how to help during a time of bereavement, so don't hesitate to tell others what you need, whether it's helping with funeral arrangements or just being around to talk. If you don't feel you have anyone you can lean on for support at this difficult time, look to widen your social network and build new friendships. Focus on those who are good listeners, but not the ones who tell you how you should be grieving or those who tell you to stop being emotionally attached to the deceased.

When you are grieving the loss of a close friend or family member, the most important thing is to feel heard by those you confide in. But the raw emotion of your grief can make some people very uncomfortable. That discomfort can cause them to avoid you, say thoughtless or hurtful things, or lose patience when you talk about your loss. Don't use their actions as a reason to isolate, though because nothing happens in a vacuum. The nature of the relationship we had with the person we are grieving, the nature of their death, and how we were taught to express our feelings all impact our grief experience. All of this combines to create a painful stew of longing, shame, guilt, loneliness and heartbreak. Turn to those who are better able to listen and provide comfort. Even when you have support from those closest to you, family and friends may not always know the best ways to help. Sharing your grief with others who have experienced similar losses can help you feel less alone in your pain. By listening to others share their stories, you can also gain valuable coping tips. To find a support group in your area, contact nearby hospitals, or call a bereavement hotline listed below. If you're struggling to accept your loss or your grief feels overwhelming, try talking to a bereavement therapist in person or someone who has experienced the same pain of loss as you.

Confiding in someone who isn't attached to your family tree or outside of your friend's circle, might help you work through emotions that may be too difficult to share with family or friends, deal with any unresolved issues from your loved one's death, and find healthier ways to adapt to life following your loss. Losing a family member, the loss of a long-term romantic partner or spouse can be especially challenging. The surviving partner may have to deal with a multitude of decisions regarding funeral arrangements, finances, and more, at what feels like the worst possible time to have to deal with such matters. The bereaved partner may also have to explain the death to children and help them through their grief. The death of one's child, regardless of the cause of death or the age of the child, is an emotionally devastating event that can overwhelm a parent. Losing your child may arouse an overwhelming sense of injustice for lost potential, unfulfilled dreams, and senseless suffering. Parents may even feel responsible for the child's death. They may also feel that they have lost a vital part of their own identity. The death of a parent has a deep impact no matter what age a person is when it occurs. It is only natural to feel consumed by a combination of pain, fear, regrets, and deep sadness at such a significant loss. The specifics of how one grieves will depend on a number of personal factors, including one's relationship with the parent, religious beliefs, previous experience with death, and whether or not one believes it was time for the parent to die. The loss of a parent may also mean the loss of a lifelong friend, counsellor, and adviser.

When you are grieving the loss of a loved one, days feels the same and sometimes it can feel like you are going through the same process over and over again. Everyday you wake up from bed, and think about the deceased, the wounds of pain feel fresh as if they've been reopened. The pain of loss of like a fresh knife cut wound, each time it's exposed to salt, it always feels as painful as the first time it happened. Therefore, the bereaved person may suddenly feel very much alone, even with the support of other family and friends. Because the loss of a loved one is an inevitable part of life, and grief is a natural part of the healing process. The reasons for grief are many, such as the loss of a loved one, the loss of health, or the letting go of a long-held dream.

Dealing with a significant loss can be one of the most difficult times in a person's life. Talking to someone who has dealt with loss in the past can help you identify new ways of coping. Only you know what works best with your personality and lifestyle. One way to examine your own style of coping is to recall the ways you've dealt with painful times in the past. It's important to note that some ways of coping with grief are helpful, like talking to others or writing in a journal. Others may be hurtful or destructive to the healing process, like abusing substances or isolating yourself. Healthy coping skills are important in resolving a loss and helping you move forward in the healing process. But also keep in mind that, the length of the grief process is different for everyone.

There is no right or wrong way of grieving, just like

there's no predictable schedule for grief. Although it can be quite painful at times, the grief process should not be rushed. It is important to be patient with yourself as you experience your unique reactions to the loss.

With time and support, things generally do get better. However, it is normal for significant dates, holidays, or other reminders to trigger feelings related to the loss. Taking care of yourself, seeking support, and acknowledging your feelings during these times are ways that can help you cope. Not everyone grieving asks for support, you just find a way that works for you and stick to that just like I found my own way of dealing with my endless grieving process which is to write exactly how I feel about a certain situation or whenever I have a question, I wish I could've asked my late mother. I found peace in her death and decided not to let that ruin my life. I am not superman or someone possessed with supernatural qualities. As we work to balance our inner and outer worlds, we may be surprised to discover that each of us grieves differently, even among siblings one may grieve with many tears and the other with none. One may feel supported in a group, the other may crave time alone with their grief. Without being aware of it, some of us tend to feel that our way of grieving is the right way. We think others should grieve as we do. Regardless of the grief we feel, we usually fall toward one end of the pendulum or the other. We are either "grieving the right way or our way or judging ourselves that we are grieving the "wrong way."

In the end, we need compassion for ourselves and those around us. We have suffered a great loss in our lives, one that has shaken us to the core, and even more so if we are one of the many who lost one parent right after the other, leaving us feeling even more disconnected from the world. As we heal, we learn who we are and who our parents were in life. In a strange way, as we move through grief, healing brings us closer to the person we loved. A new relationship begins. We learn to live with the parent we lost. Now that you come to the end of life, that same life that gave you life, the memory is buried deep in your heart and dwells deep in your soul. A new relationship will continue with that parent not a physical relationship but one where the parent lives on in your heart. You will continue to remember them, think of them and love them, for the rest of your life until you meet again. Little by little, we withdraw our energy from the loss and begin to invest it back into life. We put the loss into perspective, learning how to remember our loved ones and commemorate the loss. In the days to come, as time passes, it may still hurt but in time it will hurt less frequently. All that your parent was, all the love you shared and the relationship you had will not die. That depth of love, that depth of caring, is everlasting. We can never replace our parents, but we can strengthen our family connections as we find new and deeper meaning in our existing relationships. We begin to live again, but we cannot do so until we have given grief its time. Whether our parents live near or far, are emotionally close or distant, they ground us in the world. We don't often think of them as an unseen anchor, but in truth, they hold a place in our generational timeline. They have been there since the moment we were born and even though, intellectually, we know they will die someday, how do we imagine something that has always been there, suddenly being gone?

Can you imagine a world without a sky? Of course not. It

has always been there. The death of a parent delivers us to a world we have thought about but couldn't actually fully prepare for. We are suddenly exploring new terrain, feeling rootless or as if the ground has been pulled out from under us. And in a symbolic way, it really has been. Metaphorically speaking! I am just mentally strong and I am surrounded by the fruits of my labours (my children) who remind me of how precious life is. I also found myself a jelly bean, who makes me happy by the look of their smile. When I am in her presence, I feel like someone who has never had a problem in their adult life. This doesn't imply that you should follow in my footsteps, the point exactly is that you should find your own way of doing things, you think will help you resolve any questions you might've while grieving the loss of a loved one.